HEAVYWEIGHT

ARMAGEDDON!

The Tyson-Lewis Championship Battle

SCOOP MALINOWSKI

ZUMAYA PUBLICATIONS LLC   AUSTIN TX

2008

HEAVYWEIGHT ARMAGEDDON
© 2008 by Mark "Scoop" Malinowski

ISBN 978-1-934841-16-7

Cover art and design by Angela Waters

Look for us online at
http://www.zumayapublications.com

Library of Congress Cataloging-in-Publication Data

Malinowski, Scoop, 1966-
 Heavyweight armageddon! : the Tyson-Lewis championship
battle / Scoop Malinowski.
     p. cm.
ISBN 978-1-934841-16-7 (alk. paper)
1. Tyson, Mike, 1966- 2. Lewis, Lennox, 1965- 3. Boxers
(Sports)--Biography. I. Title.
GV1132.T97M35 2008
796.830922--dc22
[B]
                        2008025043

DEDICATION

This book is dedicated to all those personify this quotate from LeRoy Neiman: "I admire a person who gives their very best effort to excel in whatever they do. And the result of that should be a benefit to others, as well as to themselves and their own example."

ACKNOWLEDGMENTS:

Thank you to Elizabeth Burton for believing in the merit of this unique tale and my ability to chronicle it. Thank you to so many people in the world of boxing for cooperation, inspiration or contribution: LeRoy Neiman, Emanuel Steward, Lennox Lewis, Harold Knight, Courtney Shand, HBO Sports, Larry Merchant, Jim Lampley, Bobby Czyz, Frank Maloney, Virgil Thrasher, Don King, Claude Abrams, Larry Goldberg, Damien Shields, Mark Taffet, Sean Sullivan, Lynn Quayle, Johnny Gonzalez, Joe Guzman, Thomas Hauser, Steve Brunt, Norman Mailer, Leon Gast, Violet Lewis, Ken Gorman, Peter Heller, Lucia Rijker, Wladimir Klitschko, Roberto Duran, Ross Greenburg, Ray Stallone, Kevin Rooney, Teddy Atlas, Hank Kaplan, Bert Sugar, Jay Mwamba, Steve Fitch, Stacy McKinley, Shelly Finkel, Wallace Matthews, George Foreman, Andrew Golota, Bernard Hopkins, Matthew E. Schapiro, Greg Juckett, Dr. Melvin Stanley, Bob

Goodman, Kelly Swanson, Bob Arum, Lee Samuels, Lou Duva, Brian Young, Seth Abraham, Michael Bentt, Arnie Boehm, Darcy Maccarone, Maureen Siman, Richard T. Slone, Kojo, Prince, Shannon Briggs, Tim Witherspoon, Renaldo Snipes, Josh Dubin, Ronnie Shields, Steve Farhood, Eddie Mustafa Muhammad, Eddie Keenan, Peter Pharoah, Brian Little, Aaron Braunstein, Drew Murray, Mike Pinto and the one who triggered my interest in boxing in 1976 with the movie *Rocky*—Sylvester Stallone.

TABLE OF CONTENTS

FOREWORD by Leroy Neiman

First Blood: Lewis and Tyson
    Meet in the Catskills   1

Tyson: Nutcase or Self Promoter?   15

Lennox: King of the Boxing Jungle   32

"I Want To Eat Your Children!"   50

Horror At The Hudson Theatre   66

Memphis Or Bust   78

Tyson Turbulence in Maui   85

Supreme and Serene in the Poconos   93

Fight Week In Memphis   111

Heavyweight Armageddon!   129

The Aftermath   163

The Future   175

Appendix 1   Tale of the Tape   199
Appendix 2   Tyson-Lewis Fight Card   201
Appendix 3   The Record of Lennox Lewis   203
Appendix 4   The Record of Mike Tyson   207
Appendix 5   Lennox Lewis Interview   213
Appendix 6   The Biofile: Lennox Lewis   219

FOREWORD

Joe Frazier, after winning the World Heavyweight title at the end of fifteen brutal rounds against Muhammad Ali in Madison Square Garden on March 8, 1971, deserved a breather. Frazier's first defense of his title was against unranked Terry Daniels the night before Super Bowl VI, January 16th, 1972, in New Orleans.

George Foreman and I were seated in Joe's corner when *Ring Magazine* publisher Bert Sugar pops up at our side.

"Seeing you two guys together, the world's number-one boxing artist and boxing's number-one contender, gives me a great idea," Bert blurts out, puffing on his cigar (smoking was still permitted in those days). "Why don't you do a collaboration feature for *Ring*?" He continued excitedly, arousing little interest. "LeRoy, you do sketches, and, George, you write a commentary."

George looks up and mutters, "What should I write?"

Bert answers briskly, "Write anything you want," and moves on in a cloud of smoke.

Smokin' Joe disposes of his challenger easily in four rounds. Immediately, Bert reappears, ready to pick up our contribution. I hand over a couple of rather uninspired sketches, as it wasn't much of a fight. At my side, George scribbles something on a sheet of paper I had torn out of my sketchbook and indifferently passes it into Bert Sugar's hands, who scans what George has written: "Anything you want."

Needless to say the article never appeared in the magazine.

In a similar manner, the foreword to this book you are about to read is a formality in which I am glad to participate. The subject of boxing is very close to my heart. Over the years, I have drawn and painted count-less fights and fighters, and the match-up in this book is an insight into the realm of heavyweight boxing and two great champions.

LeRoy Neiman
June 2008

Defense always beats attack — if
the defense is good enough.
— Jack Johnson

A champion is someone who gets
up when he can't.
— Jack Dempsey

Truth annihilates falsehood.
— African proverb

I

First Blood: Lewis and Tyson Meet in the Catskills

> The first blow is half the battle.
> — Oliver Goldsmith

> The great man is he who does not lose his child's heart.
> — Mencius

> Artistic talent is a gift from God and whoever discovers it in himself has a certain obligation to know that he cannot waste this talent—but must develop it.
> — Pope John Paul II

The night before the big fight, the troubled warrior watched karate movies and made a slew of phone calls. He called one long-time friend, just to say he felt good and everything was going to be all right, and he said, "I love you." Though if you believed everything this enigma ever said, you wouldn't know that he had any friends.

The other combatant played chess and table tennis. And watched a videotape of a fight between Mike Tyson and Frans Botha. At the end of the second round he asked that it be turned off—he knew what he needed to do.

Two great and renowned fighters, one so masterful he defeated every man he ever fought, the other so inspiring and revered one of his devoted loyalists got a full portrait of the warrior tattooed on his back along with his complete ring record down each arm.

Though they had both emerged from similarly humble and dysfunctional beginnings to achieve legendary success in professional boxing, they had evolved into completely contrasting human beings, with totally different attitudes, lifestyles and behaviors.

But the next evening, June 8, 2002, they would meet to determine who was the better man—the good one or the bad one—in what would become one of the biggest money prizefights in boxing history.

ᴄᴐ◌ᴐ

Michael Gerard Tyson was born on June 30, 1966, in Brooklyn, NY. He lived first on Herzl Street, then later Amboy Street, in Brooklyn with his mom Lorna and older siblings Rodney and Denise. Young Tyson came from a humble bed.

"You go into the heart of Brownsville and it looks like World War II hit it. The buildings aren't stable. In New York City they'd put up a new one. In Brownsville they'd leave it. Then it falls and kills people."

In the beginning, Tyson was teasingly called "fairy boy" because he wore glasses and spoke with a slight lisp. Mike remembers having few friends except his pigeons, which he kept in a coop atop an abandoned building. He would marvel at them flying in the sky, their freedom.

One day, a much older and bigger boy grabbed one of Mike's pigeons and twisted and broke its neck with his bare hands then tossed the dead bird at Mike's feet. The shy, timid boy, in an instant, uncharacteristically pounced on the bully. It was one of those moments where the course of a life changes direction

By the age of twelve, Tyson was a trouble-making terror with an adult-sized rap sheet to match his unusually massive physical presence. His mother could no longer handle him. After another visit to juvenile hall, it was decided that Mike should be removed from the streets and incarcerated at the Tryon School for Boys in the mountains of upstate Johnstown, New York. Shortly upon arriving at Tryon, Tyson learned that one of the head counselors was a former amateur and professional boxer named Bobby Stewart. Tyson told Stewart he wanted to be a fighter.

Stewart would learn that the Tyson kid had a bad reputation and, at 5 feet, 8 inches and nearly two hundred pounds, was quite a force, too. Still, the two got on well; and after less than a year together, Stewart began to wonder if he was working with something extraordinary.

"Even though he was 13, he could beat up most men." Stewart told Peter Heller for his book *Bad Intentions: The Mike Tyson Story*. "But the thing that impressed me the most was not the physical part. It was his ability to give up all the bullshit he'd done for thirteen years to devote himself to something else. The physical stuff impressed me, but the mental stuff shocked me."

Stewart became convinced Tyson was special. He knew of a man who could assess the ability and potential of this thirteen-year-old. His name was Cus D'Amato. Cus was then seventy-two. He ran a boxing gym in Catskill, NY, while living in semi-retirement after a career in boxing, most notably as the guiding force behind former Heavyweight Champion Floyd Patterson, among others.

Cus agreed to take a look. Legend has it that, to prepare Tyson for the important audition with Cus, Stewart stayed up late teaching him a few subtle moves, tricks and maneuvers that would surely be noticed and appreciated by the watchful eye of D'Amato. Mike learned, then practiced the moves late into the evening.

Then, in the middle of the night at about three a.m., the early morning silence was broken by strange noises coming from Tyson's dorm room. A couple of counselors went to the room to see what the ruckus was. When they opened the door, they found Mike—in pitch darkness—rehearsing the moves Stewart had taught him hours earlier.

The next night at Cus's gym, Tyson was ready to impress. The young machine of destruction was dazzling in two rounds of sparring. Combinations were delivered with brutal force and fascinating passion. The old man had inspired this phenomenal manchild to excel.

Moments after the session, Cus knew what he had seen. As Mike walked out of the ring, Cus said Tyson could be the next heavyweight champion of the world.

Kevin Rooney was also there that day.

"That's what Cus said," concurred Rooney, almost twenty years later in an interview we did in New York City in 2006. "'There's the next heavyweight champion of the world...if he has the interest.' I saw Mike for the first time and I thought he was lying when he said he was thirteen. I thought he was seventeen or eighteen.

"Bobby Stewart was a good boxer, a former light heavyweight. Bobby just tattooed Mike. Mike took it all. He was moving his head, he showed hand speed, and he showed the ability to punch. He had that power. Not too many guys have that one-punch knockout power. I knew this guy can't miss...if he really wanted it."

Shortly after that spectacular performance, Tyson was allowed weekend furloughs from Tryon, and by summer, it was worked out that Mike could live at the house.

"When he came to live with Cus," Rooney said, "he was still on probation. Tryon paid for his room and board for one or two years. Mike still had a probation officer who came to the house."

"He went from there to JOs [Junior Olympics]," Rooney said, "where he was like a man trapped in a boy's body. He came from the juvenile system and had that fire in his belly. That meanness. The other kids were just trying boxing, like something to try while Mike had the fire. He had the burning desire at a young age. That came from the streets, I guess. He was in and out of juvenile halls from when he was nine to thirteen. Then he comes to Cus. He didn't want to go back to the juvenile system."

D'Amato adopted Tyson and became his legal guardian when Mike was permitted to leave reform school. Future managers Jim Jacobs and Bill Cayton payed D'Amato close to a half-million dollars just to cover Tyson's living and training expenses.

"Mike was in a perfect situation. Here he was, fourteen-years-old, with the greatest boxing mind ever produced—Cus. He was just so much more advanced than everyone else. Mike used to watch old fight films every night. He loved it. He'd watch [Jack] Dempsey,

Jack Johnson, Henry Armstrong, Sugar Ray Robinson. He liked Dempsey. He used to watch Dempsey a lot. Cus told him to study the films, see what they do, see if you can learn from them. Cus would ask Mike questions after…to see if he was learning things."

In June of 1980, Tyson watched Roberto Duran win the welterweight title in 'The Brawl in Montreal' against undefeated Sugar Ray Leonard. It was a vintage performance from Duran, one of the most thrilling fighters in the history of the sport. Tyson was fascinated by the machismo of the Panamanian superstar.

"When I saw Roberto Duran fight Leonard," Tyson said in an interview years later, "I knew I wanted to be a fighter that night. His ferocity, his viciousness…he didn't care. He was, like, invincible."

After four years of small tournaments and honing his offensive and defensive skills for countless hours in the gym, Tyson entered his first national amateur boxing tournament—the National Junior Olympics at the USAF Academy in Colorado Springs, Colorado. He won his first title there when he scored three knockouts, includeing a first-round KO with a left hook to the liver against a 265-pound Hawaiian kid who fell in a massive, trembling heap.

"I often say to Mike, 'You know, I owe you a lot,' Cus said in Heller's book *Bad Intentions*. "And he doesn't know what I mean. If he weren't here, I probably wouldn't be alive today. Nature is smarter than people think. Little by little, we lose our friends that we care about, and little by little, we lose our interest. Until finally we say, What the heck am I doing here if I have no reason to go on?

"You get used to everything. Even the idea of dying is something a person gets used to. And he accepts it. I believe that people die because they no longer want to live, they have no motivation to stay alive. But I have reason with Mike here. He gives me the motivation. I will stay alive, and I will watch him become a success, because I will not leave until that happens.

"Because when I leave, he not only will know how to fight, he'll be able to take care of himself. I don't succeed when I help make a guy become champion of the world. I succeed when I help make that fellow become champion of the world and independent of me."

Hall of Fame Manager Mickey Duff remembers seeing Tyson for the first time in a tournament in New York City. He said, in *Bad Intentions*, "He paced up and down like a caged tiger, and I thought that he looked menacing. He looked like a strong kid. With not a lot of sophisticated talent yet. Natural talent, yes. But he didn't look to have any fine skills. He looked strong and awesome for his age. As I remember, he fought a kid a few years older. Knocked him out."

Years later, in 1981, Duff would bring his young twenty-two-year-old heavyweight prospect Frank Bruno to New York. Cus called Duff to arrange for the then-sixteen-year-old Tyson to spar with Bruno. Bruno, who was unbeaten and highly regarded as a huge puncher back then, was warned repeatedly to take it easy on the kid.

But this "kid," who looked like a man sculpted out of granite, swarmed all over Bruno for two rounds. Like an unstoppable force. (As fate would have it, the two would again meet some eight years later in Las Vegas for Tyson's heavyweight title.)

"I'm not a creator," D'Amato would tell reporters back then. "What I do is discover and uncover. My job is, take the spark and fan it. When it starts to become a little

7

flame, I feed it. Feed the fire until it becomes a roaring blaze. I pour huge logs on it. And then you really get a fire going. That's what I do with my boys I train. That's what I try to do."

⤜⤝

Lennox Claudius Lewis was born in London on September 2, 1965. Like Tyson's, his was not a childhood of privilege. He had one half-brother named Dennis. In his early years, he lived intermittently with his mother, his aunt and in group homes. Lewis was expelled from primary school for excessive fighting and then punching his hand through a window in the principal's office.

So he lived for a while at a boarding school in the English countryside while his mom, Violet, tried to start a new and better life in Canada. At the home, Lewis learned archery, how to play table tennis, woodworking, even had his own bicycle. Then one day, when he was about seven or eight, he put on boxing gloves.

"It was the first place I put on a pair of boxing gloves. Nobody out of the kids could fight as well as me. So, the man of the house would have to put on the boxing gloves and box with me. I can remember punching away at him, trying to hit him, but never managing to get him because he was always too big and could keep me at arm's length."

About five years later Violet Lewis was able to support her son, and Lennox moved to Lancaster Street in Kitchener, Ontario. The gangly, Cockney-accented black twelve-year-old kid with a temper soon found himself in plenty of fights.

"Lennox was very mischievous," said his mom in the book *Lennox Lewis Champion* with Ken Gorman. "He liked to fight. If he was playing with other kids, he would end up pushing, or wrestling them or hitting them. When he took up boxing, I can't imagine anyone had to teach him how to punch. He's been punching fine since he was a toddler!

"But Lennox was always very lively, but basically he was a very nice boy. He also liked to draw things. At one point I thought he'd become an architect."

Lennox first entered a boxing gym with a friend to keep an appointment with some rival youths who had agreed to settle their dispute like gentleman — with the gloves on — at Waterloo Regional Police Boxing Association gym. Though Lennox and his pal showed up, the other boys did not. Lennox decided to try boxing anyway.

That very first day, he got hit with the first punch, right smack on the nose! And he momentarily thought that boxing wasn't for him. Also, that first day, he met Arnie Boehm, who would become his coach, friend and a father figure.

Boehm, a power lineman with the local electric company and a former amateur boxer, remembered Lennox's first day when we spoke in the Poconos in 1998.

"I'd seen Lennox come in about twenty-five years ago. He was with a friend of his. They were planning a schoolyard fight. I basically told him if you came to learn how to fight, get out of my gym and don't come back. But if you want to learn to be a boxer, you found the right place.

"You could see they were both a bit nervous, but at the same time there was an eagerness about them. A boxer has got to learn the lesson of self-reliance. That's why I let beginners have a bang at each other early on. If a boy gets hurt and he says 'That's enough' he's never going to make a good boxer.

"The thing with Lennox was, sure his eyes watered

from that first punch he took on the nose. But he thought, Whoa, I've got to do something about this. And he fought back. He had heart. Even when I was showing Lennox the basics, I could see that he had a great natural talent for the sport. Ninety percent of your defense is in your stance, the way you hold your hands and position your body, where you place your feet and position your chin. He did this naturally, almost without being shown what to do.

"He was such a good pupil, so eager to learn. He was the most attentive pupil I ever had. He would look at me straight in the eye and hang on to every word I said, so eager to take in the next bit of advice. A lot of kids who wanted to be boxers would talk while I was talking or look around or fool around. But Lennox always looked me straight in the eye, hungry for what I would tell him."

Lewis won his first amateur fight by second-round KO and went undefeated for three years. He was so good, in fact, he ran out of opponents. At fifteen, he was Ontario Golden Gloves champion in the 165-lb. division. In 1980, the fifteen-year-old Lewis took on and decisioned the former Canadian amateur middleweight champion, Kingsley Hataway, who was twenty-two.

The first defeat came against Donovan Ruddock, who was three years older than Lennox at eighteen. But it was a curious and political decision, not a clear-cut one (Of course, the two would meet again twelve years later in an important WBC world title eliminator).

Even at sixteen, Lennox was showing the proper signals for a fine future in the sport.

"I first predicted Lennox would be world champion in nineteen-eighty-one, when he was sixteen," says Boehm. "The key to this man is that he doesn't like to be beaten at anything. If you beat him at anything, he'll go and practice all night. Then, the next day, he'll come back and beat you ten times in a row. That's the kind of guy he is. He doesn't like to come in second at anything."

The first major international title Lennox captured was in November 1983, where he won the gold medal in the World Junior Championships at Santo Domingo in the Dominican Republic. In front of eight thousand spectators at El Palacio de los Deportes, in temperatures nearing ninety degrees. The gold medal came by walkover over the Cuban Pedro Nemicio, who supposedly broke his hand in the semi-final. After that outstanding victory, Arnie moved Lennox up to senior division — two years before he needed to.

In January of 1984, Lennox won his first senior international bout — a 5-0 decision over a Swede named Bengt Cederquist in Stockholm.

Then came the call from Cus D'Amato. Cus had heard of Lennox's exploits and was looking for some topnotch sparring for Tyson. Boehm was aware of the old man in the Catskills and his promising heavyweight. It was the spring of 1984, the Los Angeles Olympics year, and Boehm also liked the idea of some quality sparring for his young titan. So, they agreed to train with each other for a week at the big, white painted, old nineteenth-century house at the end of the road in Catskill, New York. At that time, Lennox was considered the more advanced boxer of the two, because he had international experience and was nine months older at eighteen.

At the first meeting between Lewis and Tyson, there wasn't, as you might expect, an excess of competitive tension. In fact, the pair of phenoms actually hit it off surprisingly well, according to all witnesses. Lewis and Tyson made an odd pair: Mike was short and very stocky, Lennox was tall and skinny and quite a lanky lad back then. Lewis and Tyson did many things those first few days, such as training together in the gym, running up the mountains, competing to see who was stronger and who could do more pushups or bench presses. They watched fight films on the old movie projector up in Mike's room.

"He'd show me dirty tricks some guys would play," Lewis remembered. "He showed me fights that were meaningful to his life."

Mike also showed Lennox his pigeons. They ate together at the house. And, of course, they talked about girls.

On day three, Cus wanted them to spar. Now, more than two decades later, there are still conflicting opinions on who won. "They're joking like the best of pals," said Boehm. "Then, when Cus rings the bell, suddenly everything changed. Tyson comes tearing across the ring like a tiger. Mike became an animal. Lennox was not prepared for that. He caught Lennox by surprise, and he put quite a number on Lennox. So, the first round was kind of a disaster for Lennox. Lennox had a bloody nose and so on. The first round went to Tyson.

"Lennox came to the corner, I cleaned him up. I said, Look, we don't have to do this today. He said, 'Oh, no, I know what to do now.' So, the second round starts, and Lennox is boxing well, sticking and moving. In fact, sometimes he'd even dodge and run to get away from Tyson, because he wasn't accustomed to that kind of ferociousness. So, the first day was all Mike."

Lennox remembers the sparring.

"Definitely, he did better that first day. I wasn't expecting his type of sparring. I'm thinking more like it's a sport. Score points, hit and don't be hit. He's thinking he wants to take my head off.

"Tyson helped me. Until then I thought of it as a sport. He brought more violence to it. I realized if I'm not careful, he can hurt me. After the first day, it was a Frazier-Muhammad Ali thing. Me boxing and moving, scoring from the outside, and him using those quick combinations and that quick head movement that he *had*.

"I put on my Muhammad Ali routine for him. I started dancing around the ring, and every time he got close to me, I held him and closed him down. He was very strong and busy. I remember that he was so strong, yet he was younger than I was. What bothered him most about me was, I wouldn't stand there and just get hit. When a man's trying to hit you, you've got to use up the whole ring. I was dancing like Ali. He couldn't catch me. And it made him angry.

"I remember one time Mike couldn't get to me. And he opened up his gloves and showed me his chin, like, eggin' me on, daring me to hit him. And I fired back five punches. I hit him with five punches and bloodied his lip. And I still remember what Cus yelled. 'Mike, What are you doing? Don't be droppin' your hands with this guy! Don't do that!'"

"It was competitive sparring," Rooney recalled. "No knockdowns or anything. Nothing special. I think Mike more than held his own."

After the sparring was finished, Cus immediately realized a prophecy — one that would come true eighteen years later. "The greatest boxing mind ever produced" remarked, "You two will meet again in the ring someday."

II

Tyson: Nutcase or Self Promoter?

Nothing is so cruel as a man raised
from lowly station to prosperity.

—Claudian

After the Catskill sparring, Lewis and Tyson would not
see one another for many years. Tyson, unexpectedly,
got knocked off the US Olympic Team after losing decisions in the Olympic Trials and Box-offs to Henry
Tillman, who would later win Olympic heavyweight
gold in Los Angeles. Lewis qualified for Canada in the
super-heavyweight division and won his first match by
third-round TKO over Pakistan's Mohammad Yousuf.

But Lennox's next match was scheduled against the
tournament favorite, Tyrell Biggs, the reigning world
amateur champion, who had only six losses in 109 bouts.
The much more experienced Biggs won by decision.

After the Olympics, while Lewis somewhat surprisingly declined substantial money offers to turn pro in
order to gain more international amateur seasoning,

Tyson joined the pro ranks on March 6, 1985. His debut was a smashing first-round KO over Hector Mercedes in Albany, NY.

Tyson's career was managed astutely by longtime D'Amato associates Jim Jacobs and Bill Cayton, who both operated the world's largest fight film company, The Big Fights, Inc. Very quickly, Tyson would assert himself on the professional level, scoring nineteen knockouts in the first twelve months of his career. Jacobs and Cayton helped create buzz and exposure for Mike by sending a custom-made video parade of Tyson knockouts to all the major print and TV media outlets.

But on November 4, 1985, Team Tyson suffered a devastating blow. Cus D'Amato died of pneumonia. This was traumatic for Tyson. The man who had saved his life was gone.

"I miss him as much as ever," Tyson would say years later. "It's no easier now than when Cus died. I'm still coverin' up the hole that Cus left in me. Cus was everything to me. He was like a father, a friend, my mentor, my trainer. I lost all that."

"Cus cared about Mike," Kevin Rooney said. "And making him successful. No one talked bad about Cus or any of his fighters. Cus had a master plan—get Mike enough experience, then turn pro. Then, when he became champion, the plan was for Mike to be a classy champion—like Cus's other champions Floyd Patterson and Jose Torres. But then Cus died after Mike's eleventh pro fight, Don King came along and the rest is history."

Only nine days after Cus passed away, Tyson stopped Eddie Richardson in fifty-eight seconds—his twelfth win. Richardson was asked if he was ever hit harder.

"Yeah, about a year ago," he replied. "I was hit by a truck."

By his twenty-eighth pro fight, Tyson was the youngest heavyweight champion in history at age twenty when he stopped Trevor Berbick in the second round in Las Vegas. To celebrate, Tyson and his pals went to see Redd Foxx perform later that evening. When Tyson returned home in New York, he poured a bottle of champagne on D'Amato's grave.

Tyson's championship reign was extraordinary. He transcended the sport like perhaps only one or two other heavyweight champions in history. His media sound bites were as unforgettable as his ring performances.

"How dare these boxers challenge me with their primitive skills?"…"I try to catch him right on the tip of the nose because I try to push the bone into the brain."…"I just want them to keep bringing guys on, and I'm going to strip them of their health. I bring pain, lots of pain."

Iron Mike earned millions upon millions through ring earnings and endorsements with Pepsi, Suntory beer and Nintendo, among others, and he became one of the most recognizable men on the planet. He had a TV contract with HBO that put him among the wealthiest television entertainers in America, narrowly behind Bill Cosby and Johnny Carson.

But the zenith was approaching, and the imminent downfall. While Tyson's success reached staggering heights, his out-of-the-ring problems began to escalate.

Historian Bert Sugar remembers Tyson back in these early days: "Oh, he was the sweetest guy I ever met. He was just nice, very deferential, very quiet. Then somehow, someway, somewhere, something else kicked in.

"Cus had introduced me to him. At this point, I asked

Jimmy Jacobs, who was really his manager, Why is Mike fighting so often? To keep him out of trouble. Then it began to occur to me why."

Don King and the actress Robin Givens emerged into Tyson's universe at this time. As his personal life began to unravel, his domination of the ring began to suffer a gradual dissipation, particularly after the passing of co-manager Jim Jacobs to leukemia at age fifty-eight and the eventual firing of Kevin Rooney. After he had so magically fulfilled Cus D'Amato's prediction by winning the World Heavyweight Championship, Tyson's world slowly started to collapse.

In June of 1987, Tyson was charged with assault after he allegedly struck a parking lot attendant who had intervened after Tyson had tried to kiss a female employee. Tyson later settled out of court. In August, Iron Mike won a decision over Tony Tucker to take the International Boxing Federation title that unified all three belts for him.

In January 1988 he stopped former champ Larry Holmes in four rounds. In February, he married Robin Givens. Later that year, Givens's sister and mother accused Tyson of physical beatings.

In March, Mighty Mike knocked out Tony Tubbs in two rounds at Tokyo. On June 27, Tyson, perhaps at the very pinnacle of his career, obliterated unbeaten Michael Spinks in one minute and thirty-one seconds in Atlantic City, NJ. In August, he broke a bone in his right hand during a four a.m. street fight with boxer Mitch "Blood" Green outside Dapper Dan's clothing store in Harlem.

Two weeks later, Tyson was hospitalized after being knocked unconscious as a result of driving his BMW into a tree in upstate New York. Previously, in May, on the way home to New Jersey with Givens and her mother in the car, Tyson drove his $180,000 silver Bentley into a parked car in Manhattan. There were varying accounts as to what caused the strange collision: Tyson supposedly was trying to avoid hitting a stray cat, Tyson was being hit by his wife. According to several accounts, Tyson and Givens were arguing, and when she began slapping him, the heavyweight champion lost control of the car. Tyson told the arriving police officers they could keep the automobile, adding, "I've had nothing but bad luck and accidents with this car."

But Iron Mike's bad luck had only just begun. On September 30, 1988, Tyson and his wife appeared on national TV with ABC's Barbara Walters at their north New Jersey mansion. In the bizarre interview, Robin admitted she feared him.

"Michael is manic depressant," Givens stated to the ABC cameras. She said Mike had a scary side and "he shakes, he pushes, he swings." On October 2, police had to rush to Tyson's Bernardsville, NJ, home after he hurled furniture out the window, scaring Robin and mother-in-law Ruth Roper enough to flee the property. Just a week later, the marriage would end when Givens filed for divorce.

In December, a woman sued Tyson for allegedly grabbing, propositioning and insulting her at a night club. Tyson later was found guilty of battery and fined $100.

Despite all the personal turmoil, he still somehow managed to keep his focus when it came to boxing. The Tyson-Givens divorce was finalized on February 14, 1989, in the Dominican Republic. Only eleven days later, Tyson defended his title for the eighth time by stopping old sparring partner Frank Bruno in the fifth round.

Bruno said, after the loss, "He's got nuclear-powered fists."

In April, Tyson was again accused of slapping a parking lot attendant outside a Los Angeles night club after the attendant asked him to remove his Mercedes Benz from a spot reserved for the club's owner. Charges were later dropped. In July, in what would be the final win of his unbeaten title reign, Tyson stopped Carl "The Truth" Williams in the first round.

King Tyson's empire finally would come crashing down in Tokyo in February 1990. Vic Zeigel, a columnist for the *New York Daily News* was there, and he was not entirely astonished by the result.

"Did you ever pick a winner off what you saw at a press conference? Tyson was never very good at press conferences, and he was especially bad at this one — pretending to be asleep, lazy answers, etc. Buster Douglas, though, was terrific. After coming out of the room, I asked the other writers, If you didn't know one of these guys was a huge underdog, who would you pick in this fight based on what you saw and heard back there? To a man, they answered Buster."

Lacking his old energy and passion, Tyson lost the richest, most coveted prize in sport to the 42-1 underdog named James "Buster" Douglas of Columbus, Ohio. A tenth-round right uppercut was the deathblow. It still ranks as one of the most stunning upsets in sporting history.

Four months later, in June, Tyson returned by scoring a first-round KO of his former amateur rival Henry Tillman. In December, he scored another first-round KO over Alex Stewart. In March of '91, he defeated Donovan "Razor" Ruddock by TKO 7. In June of '91 Tyson horrified reporters when he launched into a bizarre rant against Ruddock, claiming, "I'm gonna make him my girlfriend," calling Ruddock "a transvestite" and adding, "I can't wait for you to kiss me with those big lips of yours." On June 28, he won a violent, hard-fought decision over Ruddock.

The loss of the D'Amato influence and the "gain" of Don King as his promoter and new central father figure were certainly having a profound influence on Tyson's attitude, behavior and manners. Then Tyson's lawless conduct finally reached the point of no return.

On July 18, 1991, in Indianapolis, Tyson met eighteen-year-old Miss Black America beauty contestant Desiree Washington. Four days later, Washington would accuse the ex-champ of having raped her in room 606 of the Canterbury Hotel. In September of '91, Tyson was indicted by a special Indiana grand jury on rape and three other charges. Then, in February of '92, after nine hours of deliberations, he was found guilty of rape and two counts of deviate sexual conduct. He was sentenced to six years at Indiana Youth Center by Marion County Superior Court Judge Patricia Gifford.

◌⊙◌

While Tyson was dominating boxing, making headlines and ultimately self-destructing, Lennox Lewis concentrated on preparing to win the gold medal in the 1988 Olympic Games in Seoul, Korea. He earned gold at the Commonwealth Games in 1986. Though he did fine-tune his skills and acquired valuable international experience, he lost a few key fights to Ulli Kaden, Jorge Luis Gonzalez and Alexander Morisnichenko, all by decision.

But Lewis would later avenge all of those defeats, a foreshadowing of how he would administer future setbacks in his pro career. By the time of the Olympics, he felt primed and ready after four years of preparations, and was one of the favorites along with the American Riddick Bowe and the German, Kaden. Lennox won his first match inside of one round over a Kenyan. Then he surprised many in the quarter-finals by stopping Kaden in just thirty-four seconds. Kaden had decisioned Lewis the previous autumn in the World Cup in Belgrade.

Next up was Poland's Janusz Zarenkiewicz in the semis, but the Pole pulled out, claiming a hand injury, giving Lennox the benefit of an extra rest before the gold medal final against Bowe. The night before that match, Lewis watched an interview with Bowe on TV. Bowe spoke with boastful overconfidence as though it were a mere formality for him to go and dispose of Lewis the next day, pick up his gold medal and then seek out the then-still unbeaten Mike Tyson in the professional ranks. This was all the extra motivation the focused and driven Lewis needed. How careless of Bowe, to treat his rival as just an insignificant afterthought.

It would turn out to be quite a foolish misjudgment. Though he started slow in the bout, absorbing three right uppercuts from Bowe, one of which bloodied his nose, Lewis got down to business in the next round. He rushed out of the corner and assailed his foe. Bowe was in trouble from the bell. A five-punch combination sent him back into the ropes for a standing-eight count. Another looping right and left ended matters after forty-three seconds of the round, and Canada had its first boxing gold medal since the 1932 Olympics when Horace Gwynne won bantamweight honors.

Lewis, the new Olympic hero, was never forgetful of the influence that his first coach Arnie Boehm had on him.

"Arnie was instrumental in my life," Lewis said in

the book *Lennox Lewis Champion* with Ken Gorman. "And without his blessing and without his tutelage, I wouldn't be who I am today. He made me, basically, into a man. He took me camping. He gave me money to go roller-skating. He bought me my first head gear and my first jock. He taught me how to drive a car. Anything that I've accomplished in my life is because of him. He was my friend, father figure, coach and mentor. He had everything to do with what I became and what I will become."

After the Olympic triumph, Lewis needed to find proper management to guide his professional career. The most prominent candidates attempted to court him, including Stan Hoffman, Bob Arum, Emanuel Steward and the Duva family. Surprisingly, Lewis eventually opted to hire a little-known British manager named Frank Maloney.

Lewis decided to move back home to East London from Toronto and became a British-based heavyweight.

"I could have fought in America," he said. "But I think this is something I wanted to do. I grew up in East London and I'm from England and it was the best route for me to take."

Lewis commenced his pro career on June 27, 1989, with a second-round KO over Al Malcolm in London. With most of his early fights in England, he did not generate much fanfare outside of Europe. His progress was low-key and steady but nothing earth-shattering like Tyson's in 1985 and '86. Though Lennox scored twenty-one straight wins over four years — with eighteen KO's — there were more than a few expert observers who believed he was being mismanaged. Hall of Fame boxing manager Mickey Duff was publicly critical of Maloney's guidance, saying he's "...doing a Cecil B. DeMille in reverse...they're taking a star and turning him into an unknown."

Despite the criticisms, Lewis and his team were well on their way to the top of the mountain. Though still largely an unknown heavyweight in America, Lewis's first major test and breakout fight came against old nemesis Donovan "Razor" Ruddock. The fight was set for Halloween night 1992 at the Royal Albert Hall in London, to be televised back in the States by HBO. Most important, the winner of this fight would meet the winner of the forthcoming Bowe-Evander Holyfield title fight. At the time, Holyfield was undisputed champion after defeating Buster Douglas in 1990.

Against the most dangerous adversary of his pro career, at age twenty-six, Lewis was simply devastating. In the first round, an uncomfortable-looking Ruddock started poorly. He attempted a lazy, pawing jab. Lewis saw his opening and detonated Ruddock swiftly with a missile of a right. Ruddock flopped heavily to the floor but was saved by the bell.

In round two, Lewis immediately went on the attack. To his credit, Ruddock fought back bravely and desperately, but Lewis showed his class was in another league as he quickly finished the job with a vicious assault of accurate punches.

Ruddock had been completely destroyed in the first minute of the second round. The jubilant British audience was ecstatic. There was a sense of discovery in the air as everyone realized that Lennox Lewis was not just another good but not special British heavyweight. He was going to be a superstar.

This was a startling performance by Lewis because Ruddock—coming off two competitive losses to Tyson—was considered the best heavyweight currently not imprisoned. Unfortunately for Ruddock, the loss was so shattering he would never again be a factor in heavy-weight boxing. For Lewis, this was just the beginning.

Larry Merchant of HBO was uncharacteristically high-pitched in lauding the performance. "We have a great new heavyweight on the boxing scene," Merchant announced on the air. "Lennox Lewis may turn out to be not only the greatest heavyweight in British history but the greatest fighter in European history."

His broadcast partner, George Foreman, concurred emphatically. "I agree, I agree! There's nothing in the world that can stop this young man but himself. If he keeps his feet on the ground, he can become a good champion. He had a good left, more than we expected tonight. He had a good overhand right but also a left hook that really dropped him the last time."

The sad truth is that Lewis was too impressive for his own good. Bowe, fresh off of decisioning Holyfield, would refuse to honor his promised agreement to fight Lewis. He would eventually dump the WBC belt into a trashcan during a publicity stunt at a London hotel when he knew the WBC was going to strip him anyway. Bowe did not actually leave the belt in the garbage—he would still take the memento with him.

So, Lewis actually earned a portion of the World Heavyweight title—while he was on vacation in Jamaica.

Consequently, Lewis's "winning" the title in such a manner would actually hurt his reputation in the long run, as it kind of overshadowed the plain truth that Bowe had, indeed, ducked him. It took Lewis many years to correct the false impression that he was just a paper champion who was handed the title.

But make no mistake about it—Bowe and his manager Rock Newman were very shrewd, and they were fully aware of the extreme risks involved in a fight with Lewis. They simply were not up to the challenge.

Meanwhile, Tyson was still jailed in Indiana; he would end up serving three years of a six-year sentence. Good behavior cut his time in half, though there were reports that he could have been released earlier had he admitted to and apologized for his crimes. Tyson, however, vowed never to admit to raping Washington because he still insisted he really never did it. Yet, according to some people who knew him, Mike felt he somewhat deserved to be in jail after all, because he privately confessed that he was guilty of having done worse things than raping Washington at other times in his life.

Tyson's prison sentence ended on March 25, 1995. At approximately six a.m., in the freezing morning darkness, Mike Tyson, wearing a dark Muslim outfit and white prayer cap, became a free man again. At his side were his old promoter Don King, boyhood chums Rory Holloway and John Horne and an attractive woman named Monica Turner. Also on hand were hundreds of reporters and photographers from all over the globe.

King blocked their view of Tyson. As it turned out, he had already made a special deal with Showtime network for the first TV interview and pictures of the freed Tyson. Just as the convoy assembled into their limousines to depart, a group of Muslims representing Louis Farrakhan arrived on the scene, but King was able to make the escape...with the prized boxer in his clutches.

When Tyson was in jail he had received many visitors. Some of the top players of the sport—or their agents or messengers—came to make proposals and offers. Rock Newman and Riddick Bowe tried to interest Tyson in an all-Brooklyn superfight to be held at Madison Square Garden. Matthew Saad Muhammad, a former WBC light heavyweight champion and a boxing hero of Tyson's, made several trips to Indianapolis from his home in Pleasantville, NJ, apparently as the envoy of the Muslim group.

Tyson in prison was free game. The prevailing school of thought was that he would never in a thousand years go back with King, who had allegedly bilked him out of millions while he was incarcerated.[1] There were even crazy whispers that King had designed for Tyson to be set up and convicted of rape so as to loot his finances. This seemed a bit fantastic, but the fact that King had hired a tax lawyer named Vince Fuller to defend Tyson against the rape charges was mystifying to some legal experts.

Tyson called a press conference at the Gund Arena in Cleveland five days later. His ability to shock would be in evidence once again.

"There's been a lot of speculation about my plans," he said, reading from a prepared statement. "Here they are. I will fight again. I want to confirm John Horne and Rory Holloway as my co-managers. I also want to confirm that Don King continues to be my promoter. Don is the greatest promoter in the world."

King had done it again. He had scored exclusive control over one of the world's most famous, most alluring sporting attractions.

But it was not so easy this time. Stories were going around about how King had to supposedly beg, plead and even cry on his knees for Tyson to take him back.

Don King now had full control over Tyson's career...again. This bewildered and frustrated many insid-

---

[1] Tyson's 1998 $100 million lawsuit against King was settled for around $10-15 million in 2004.

ers, as Tyson was still the biggest entity in boxing. Every promoter, every major network, every major Las Vegas casino clamored for his services.

And Tyson had all the leverage. He didn't have to sign away his future to just one promoter like King, or anybody else. He could have sat back, fight by fight, and watched as rival promoters drove up his value against each other in heated bidding wars. It's called maximizing your opportunity as a free agent. Sugar Ray Leonard, Roy Jones and Muhammad Ali each have deftly managed their careers under this strategy. Tyson, perhaps the biggest moneymaker of them all, was in the perfect position to do the same. But he gave it all away to King.

Hall of Fame promoter Dan Duva, now deceased, summed it up best.

"Why would anyone expect him to come out smarter? He went to prison for three years, not Princeton."

King, of course, would take full advantage of his machinations. He secured a six-fight deal with the MGM Grand through 1997, though no figures were ever announced. Sources estimated the deal's worth, which included stock options, in the $100-200 million range.[2]

During his incarceration, Tyson began studying Islam with a prison Imam named Muhammad Siddeeq. There were rumors Tyson contemplated a name change to Malik Abdul Aziz (Malik means *king* or *ruler*, Abdul Aziz means *servant of the almighty*). He got tattoos of Mao Tse Tung, Che Guevara and Arthur Ashe. Of his stint behind bars, Tyson said he spent countless hours read-

---

[2] Years later King bragged on national television of his paying over $32 million in taxes on one year of income — not once but twice. It is assumed that these Tyson years were the prime of King's earning career, as he had no other meal tickets anywhere near as lucrative as Tyson.

ing authors like Voltaire, Dumas, Machiavelli and Maya Angelou. His outlook on life seemed to mature.

"I chose to be that person locked up," he said in *Boxing Update* newsletter. "We get to write our own book in life. I don't choose to do that anymore. In prison, I was discovering what I was really about and I found out that I was a pretty decent person. I kinda like myself. I never liked myself before. That's how come I didn't care if I got killed. Because I was trying to kill myself without putting a gun to my head. The way I was living...I wanted to die. I didn't care. But as I got to know myself, I started liking myself."

His childhood pal and now co-manager, Rory Holloway said the experience of jail benefited Tyson.

"Mike's a different human being. He is very humble. He has grown into a man."

Tyson had also grown into a bigger entertainment attraction than ever before. The hugely anticipated comeback of Iron Mike was set for August 20, 1995, at the MGM Grand in Las Vegas. Showtime's SET Pay-Per-View would televise the scheduled ten-rounder. On top of the gigantic MGM deal, King had also scored another huge multi-million dollar pact with Showtime.

After more than four years of boxing inactivity, the twenty-nine-year-old Tyson scored a first-round KO over unknown and unheralded Peter McNeeley. But the win was inconclusive, as Tyson missed his ample and stationary target with an alarming amount of errant punches. The stoppage came when McNeeley's trainer climbed up to the ring apron and waved surrender.

For the eighty-nine-second win, Tyson's paycheck was not as sloppy. He earned an incredible $25 million.

∽∾

Lewis defended his WBC title twice in 1993 against Tony Tucker (W12) and Frank Bruno (TKO 7). Next up, he disposed of Phil Jackson in seven rounds in May of '94. Meanwhile, Bowe and Holyfield were ignoring a fight with him, and perhaps Lewis grew bored to some degree at not getting the opportunity to star in a marquee superfight event. As the saying goes, "Great fighters have trouble getting up for mediocre fights."

The idols of the sport only become defined as great by having their skills tested and their fortitude threatened, like Ali with Frazier, Norton and Foreman, Leonard with Duran, Robinson with LaMotta, Louis with Schmeling.

"Prowess without an adversary shrivels" — a quotation from the Latin philosopher Seneca.

Lewis, believing he was the best, aspired to prove his mettle against the most dangerous fighters the world had to offer. He was tired of meaningless fights that proved little. He wanted to be challenged by someone who could bring out his ultra-best. He wanted the chance to shine in a superfight, as Pete Sampras demonstrated his finest tennis shot-making at Wimble-don, not in Scottsdale or Rotterdam.

So, on September 24, 1994, disaster would strike him. It came in the form of the right hand from the little-known former Tyson sparring partner and number-one World Boxing Council contender Oliver "The Atomic Bull" McCall. Lewis went down in round two, rose on wobbly legs and was waved out of the fight by referee Lupe Garcia.

The new WBC champion McCall was, of course, promoted by Don King. And with Tyson back on the boxing scene, this was another spectacular boon for that lucky devil King, because this meant he now had control of one of the heavyweight titles again. He had not enjoyed that kind of superlative power since Tyson lost to Douglas in 1990. McCall's win over Lewis meant King now could match Tyson in a title fight with one of his own fighters.

This was a crushing, devastating setback for Lewis. Even as champ, no one had done him any favors. And there certainly would be no favors coming now.

Any hopes of a Lewis-Tyson match would have to wait...and wait.

III

Lennox: King of the Boxing Jungle

> The strongest man on earth is he who
> stands most alone.
> — Henrik Ibsen

> When a true genius appears in the
> world, you may know him by this
> sign; that the dunces are all in con-
> federacy against him.
> — Jonathan Swift

> To be great is to be misunderstood.
> — Ralph Waldo Emerson

For Lewis, the one-punch defeat by Oliver McCall was the first time he had ever been knocked out in his amateur or pro career. Such a failure can be traumatic for a fighter. It is a humiliation in front of a global audience. All the other heavyweights watched it and gained from it. Now they all knew Lewis was vulnerable and capable of being destroyed.

Any boxer who has been knocked out has to face a difficult question. He must choose—either abandon his dream, or pick up the broken pieces and put them all back together again. Confidence must be rebuilt. Doubt must be extinguished. Fear of being hit hard again must be overcome. Momentum of a rising career must be regained. Aura and reputation must again be constructed all over again. It is hard enough as it is to enter into the profession of being a prizefighter, to fight for survival. But to get destroyed physically and psychologically by another man, and then to come back from that kind of adversity, is an ultimate act of courage.

The first step is the difficult self-analysis process — to figure out the reasons why, exactly, the knockout occurred — then make the necessary corrections. A good example is the great Joe Louis, who was knocked flat on his face by Max Schmeling at the age of twenty-two in his twenty-eighth pro fight. "The Brown Bomber" studied his situation with his handlers and concluded that his training preparations were insufficient. Louis was more interested in golf outings and, allegedly, his many female visitors, rather than roadwork and sparring. In fact, one Louis biography claimed he didn't do a single round of sparring before the Schmeling loss.

Of course, Louis would make the necessary reparations to his training regimen. And two years later he returned and bested Schmeling in the first round of their epic 1938 battle at Yankee Stadium.

Some top fighters are not quite so fortunate. Joe Frazier lost the heavyweight title when he was stopped by George Foreman inside two rounds. He never won another title fight again, losing twice to Ali and four years later was again knocked out by Foreman. Michael Spinks was an unbeaten heavyweight champion, Olympic gold medalist and National Golden Gloves champion. He would never step foot into a ring again after being annihilated by Mike Tyson in just ninety-one seconds. George Foreman said it took two years to recover mentally from losing to Ali. Some wonder if it actually took much longer than that.

Former heavyweight champion Max Schmeling, who died in 2005 at age ninety-nine, believed a professional boxing career was an all-or-nothing proposition. A boxer was required to channel all of his focus and energy to his sport, or else failure would be the inevitable outcome.

"Everything became secondary to the training," Max said in his autobiography, titled *Max Schmeling: An Autobiography*, translated and edited by George Von Der Lippe. "From the very start of my career, it was clear to me that achievement was built on discipline. Accomplishment in sports demands the commitment of one's entire self...morally, intellectually and spiritually. Avoid alcohol, cigarettes, live life according to a stricter diet. A slight delay in reaction time, a letdown in exact timing, a deficient punch or the famous glass jaw can cost one a career despite all the sacrifice.

"In the ring, as elsewhere, it's intelligence that is the decisive factor. With tactics and strategy, even a less physically gifted boxer can outmaneuver a giant."

The first correction Lewis made after losing his title was the hiring of a new trainer, Emanuel Steward, to replace Pepe Correa. In boxing circles, Correa was considered a better "cheerleader" than actual boxing trainer. Lewis concluded that, under Correa's direction, he had become too robotic and stiff, and relied too much on loading up with single shots. He felt that he had actually declined from his old style of fluidity and movement, of being loose at the hips, feinting more and throwing combinations. Steward, who abruptly resigned from his training duties with new champ McCall to join with

Lewis, was quite aware of the vast arsenal inside Lennox.

"Lennox Lewis is the most talented heavyweight in the world," Steward said back in 1994 to *Boxing Update*, "but also the biggest disappointment. I am lucky that I have come across the perfect specimen for a heavyweight. In three months I will have him like I want him. My idea is to make him into a large version of Sugar Ray Robinson. Not Muhammad Ali, because I truly believe Lennox can be better than him. He can do things Ali couldn't do. Ali did not have much physical strength. Lennox can box, but he also has that tremendous, rawboned punching power. Robinson was the fighter I admired the most. Lennox can be my Sugar Ray Robinson."

Little known is the fact that Steward also received an offer from Don King to train Tyson at around this same period. King supposedly offered Steward $3,000,000 per fight to guide Tyson. But Steward chose to work with Lewis instead.

"If Lewis and Tyson ever meet, it will be a mismatch. Lennox is too good and too big for Tyson. Lennox is the most talented heavyweight in the world."

The new and improved Lewis set out to get an immediate rematch with McCall. But Don King was not at all interested in matching his new champion with Lewis, whom he had no promotional control over. King's common practice, like many other successful promoters in history, is to keep a permanent grip on his championship belts by matching his champions only against challengers he has supervision over.

Tyson, who had been released from prison while Lewis was in training at the fabled Kronk gym in Detroit with Steward, was at the forefront of King's plans. At the

WBC Annual Convention in Spain, the WBC delegates, who typically seem to make rulings that are curiously almost always in favor of King, determined that Lewis must first face heavy-hitting Don King-controlled Lionel Butler in a WBC title eliminator. If Lewis won that bout, he would get his rematch with McCall.

Or so they said. Tyson and King would have to wait for their turn at McCall until after Lewis was obliged. So those WBC delegates said.

But Lionel Butler would be a very dangerous fight for Lewis because Butler had recorded sixteen straight knockout wins, eight coming in the first round. He was on a roll. Before the fight in Sacramento, CA, King bellowed at the press conference, "Lewis has shown he ain't got no chin. Butler will destroy him. Just like McCall did!"

But Lewis was not about to make another mistake that could ruin his career. He was not to be denied. With his future on the line, he was able to avert disaster and rise to the occasion. He stopped an outclassed and gassed Butler in the fifth round.

McCall was not able to sustain any longevity as champion, though. He made one uneventful defense against the forty-five-year-old Larry Holmes at Caesars Palace in Las Vegas but lost the title by decision in his next fight against the supposedly King-controlled (via British promoter Frank Warren) Frank Bruno late in 1995 in London.

After winning the WBC title eliminator against Butler, Lewis and his team, on the other hand, now concentrated their efforts to battle Bruno, whom Lennox had already beaten by seventh-round TKO in an exciting all-British title defense in 1993.

But the WBC, in yet another blatantly pro-Don King

ruling, suddenly installed Tyson, just out of prison, as mandatory number-one contender, even though he had not fought in four years. Tyson, in effect, leapfrogged Lewis in the ratings. Bruno, predictably, was following the company line and leaning to fight Tyson.

"Lewis is merely a grain of sand on the beach," Bruno said. "Tyson is the golden nugget."

But Lewis was unwavering in his persistence to force the WBC to honor its promise—the opportunity to re-gain his title. Team Lewis even offered Bruno a whopping $7 million to face Lewis instead of Tyson. But they were rejected. It wasn't enough money, claimed Frank Warren, Bruno's promoter and a Don King ally.

Days before Bruno was set to fight Tyson in Las Vegas in March of 1996, a judge named Amos Saunders, in a Paterson, NJ, supreme courtroom said, "This fight against Mr. Bruno should have been Lennox Lewis's, not Mike Tyson's. There are some things money can't buy. Money is no compensation. There is no question he has suffered irreparable damage. I am in no doubt the WBC has treated Mr. Lewis unfairly. He was promised this fight and he should have had this fight."

Saunders accused the WBC of "making up (its) own rules" and even threatened to have the Tyson-Bruno fight postponed before finally relenting and issuing a court order that prevented Tyson and the WBC from en-gaging in a future heavyweight title fight against anyone but Lennox Lewis.

Bruno collected a purse of $6 million for losing easily to Tyson in three rounds—$1 million less than the offer from Team Lewis. Tyson, when asked about fighting Lewis after the win, was noncommittal and vague in his response.

"I will fight whoever my promoter wants me to."

King's strategy for avoiding the Lewis-Tyson fight was soon apparent. His plan was to match Tyson in a unification match with another King-promoted fighter, World Boxing Association Champ Bruce Seldon, who had won the vacant title vs. King-promoted Tony Tucker that was stripped from George Foreman.[3] Seldon was once stopped in one round by Riddick Bowe, earlier in his career. Everyone knew that it would be another easy Tyson win and another opportunity for King and Tyson to buy more time. They secretly hoped Lewis would eventually lose his patience and resolve and finally be erased from their heavyweight picture, once and for all.

Lewis, however, was determined. And he believed he was the best. He believed Tyson and King were ducking him. Eventually, Team Lewis would even offer a staggering $50 million to Tyson to fight, but King was, of course, not interested and turned it down.

It was becoming more and more clear that King had doubts about Tyson's chances against Lewis. King is no dummy. Perhaps deep down, he privately knew better than anyone that the outcome of a Lewis-Tyson match would put an emphatic end to his own stranglehold on the heavyweight title.

So, Lewis stayed active in 1995 with wins over Justin Fortune and Tommy Morrison. In May of 1996, despite the ongoing uncertainty of his supposed promised title shot, Lewis posted a grueling ten-round decision win over US Olympic gold medalist Ray Mercer.

"That, for me, was the best performance by Lennox in my time with him," Steward told the media at Madison Square Garden after the fight. "He showed he had the

---

[3] Foreman won the IBF and WBA titles from Michael Moorer who had taken them from Holyfield who had won them back in a rematch with Bowe.

balls for it. He showed he could dig deep when it really mattered. You gotta go through wars like that in your career. You have to prove that you have the resilience to fight your way through adversity. Lennox showed his chin was sound and his determination was total. He got more from that fight than from any other."

Though King and Tyson were trapped in a legal corner by Judge Saunders—box Lennox or you don't box at all—they were dead-set against a match with Lewis, regardless of the cost. King and Tyson concocted a new scheme. This time they offered Lewis $4 million to step aside and allow Tyson to fight Seldon on September 6, 1996. Also part of the deal was that Tyson's WBC title would not be at stake vs. Seldon, and Tyson was given a September '96 deadline to either commit to defending against Lewis by year's end or be stripped of the belt. Seldon, like a puppet, agreed easily to all terms, including defending his title against Tyson, even though Tyson's WBC belt would not be at stake.

It is true Lewis accepted the largest step-aside payment in boxing history. It was a shrewd but a much-criticized maneuver. Some of the American media criticized him for this decision, especially Ron Borges of the *Boston Globe*, who wrote: "Lewis's men took the money because they never wanted the fight in the first place... Lewis is a man without pride or any sense of self...Lennox Lewis is as phony as his British citizenship papers."

The bottom line is, Lewis earned $4 million for just waiting what only figured to be an additional four months to finally get to fight Tyson.

Predictably, Tyson destroyed Seldon easily in one round for the WBA title. And afterwards, Tyson—surprise!—relinquished the WBC title. He did not want to fight Lewis. Instead, he had his sights set on an opponent deemed to be safer than Lewis—Evander Holyfield.

But Lewis was not put at a total loss by this development. All the time and dollars spent on legal fees and court wrangling had put him in position to fight for the Tyson-vacated WBC title, against none other than his old nemesis, the King-promoted Oliver McCall.

Ever since defeating Lewis with his right hand two-and-a-half years earlier, McCall's life collapsed in disarray. He now allegedly had a severe drug problem. Three times in 1996 alone he was arrested for possession of drugs and violence. In one incident, McCall threw a Christmas tree in a hotel lobby and spat on a police car as police took the former champion into custody.

Regardless, Lewis-McCall II would happen. How a fighter was permitted to enter a boxing match, not to mention the honor of participating in a World Heavyweight title fight, with such a glaringly obvious personal problem, is a shame on the people who allowed it to happen.

Still, McCall, with his one-punch KO power and with Don King at his side, was a dangerous threat for Lewis, drugs or no drugs. At the opening bell, McCall charged Lewis like a wild animal.

But Lewis was ready this time. He jabbed and boxed masterfully, unloading a vicious beating on poor McCall. "The Atomic Bull," who had worked some three hundred rounds with Tyson without ever being knocked down, had a jaw as durable as titanium, but by the third round, it was apparent McCall did not have the mental fortitude to defeat Lewis for a second time. He suddenly began crying, turned his back on Lewis and walked away.

At the bell, McCall refused to return to his corner to Georgie Benton, electing to stroll around the ring while crying and making facial gestures to the confused audience. By the fifth round, referee Mills Lane had seen enough and disqualified McCall for "refusing to fight."

"I could not accept it as a good victory because it was overshadowed by his behavior," admitted Lewis in *Lennox Lewis Champion*. "I even felt a bit sorry for him, but not a lot. I don't cry for McCall. He created his own problems. That's his destiny, he chose that road. My career was in the wilderness for two-and-a-half years. But I didn't crack up."

Lewis had finally regained the WBC championship, but the achievement was overshadowed again, this time by McCall's nutty antics. So, the general perception of Lewis as a World Heavyweight Champion by the media and the fans was far less than it really should have been.

On the other hand, Mike Tyson, despite winning all of his comeback matches by stoppage, had been, to the experienced eye, distinctly unimpressive in his post-incarceration version. His opposition of McNeeley, Seldon, Bruno and Buster Mathis Jr. all seemed to know their secondary status and came to submit to Tyson.

Even then, with such mediocre opposition in front of him, Tyson looked clumsy on his feet, his timing seemed off and his punches were just not nearly as sharp, accurate or as overwhelming as they had used to be. Unchallenging opposition, overindulgent lifestyle and maybe even marriage (in April 1997, to Dr. Monica Turner) may have had some effect on Tyson's boxing prowess.

Despite the evident flaws, Tyson was still a hugely potent brand name, and King was taking every precaution to keep his asset safe from any adverse risk. Dangerous opposition like Lennox Lewis was to be avoided. So, the next choice of an opponent for Tyson was the perceived "over-the-hill" Evander Holyfield.

Holyfield was now thirty-four, and coming off a TKO loss to Bowe and an unspectacular win over former cruiserweight champion Bobby Czyz. He was a 22-1 underdog when the fight was first announced. Some experts even feared for Holyfield's health. To King and Tyson, however, Holyfield's well-being did not matter. He was a marquee name and the perfect choice as the next "sacrificial lamb" for the monster Tyson.

But at the initial press conference to publicize the fight, Holyfield would make it clear he was not coming to play second banana to Tyson. And he was not intimidated by Tyson, not in any way. In fact, Holyfield fully intended on whupping the baddest man on the planet, and his statement to the media was absolutely fascinating to listen to.

"Tyson might frighten [the media], but he doesn't scare me," he explained matter-of-factly, with Tyson sitting a just few chairs away on the dais. "This is my game, my trade. I've been everywhere he has except prison. You can't just outbox him. You have got to be prepared to fight.

"The point is, that to beat a guy like that, you've got to fight him to get his respect, and then box him. If he puts you in a corner, you have to fight. If you have space, then you can box. You have to do both. And if a guy can't fight, he's not going to win. I'm ready for November ninth. I want to be champion of the world again.

"Everybody hypes Tyson up to be the man. We all know what fear is. But Tyson knows he's going in with a guy who isn't afraid of him. He knows I've been through a lot of adversity, same as him. But all big punchers are affected when they get hit. They're used to doing the hitting, and I don't think Tyson's the sort of guy to get up when he goes down."

At this point, an upset Tyson suddenly rose from his seat and shouted at Holyfield, "You got nothing coming on November ninth, nothing! I'm gonna enjoy this fight. I can't wait till November ninth!"

Clearly, Holyfield's bold speech had hit a nerve, and Tyson could not conceal his irritation. Holyfield's reference to Tyson not being able to get up when he went down was a stinging reminder of the Buster Douglas fight, when Tyson went crashing to the canvas from the uppercut and was not able to make it to his feet in time to continue. Finally, Tyson would be facing his first real challenge since being released from prison. Holyfield, for sure, had the self-belief and the experience to challenge Mike Tyson both physically and psycho-logically.

It turned out to be a classic confrontation, a wildly exciting battle that Tyson was not equipped to deal with. Holyfield entered the ring with a knowing smile. The former champ would absorb Tyson's best punches and continually overpower him throughout the match, pushing and shoving the bully around the ring. The end came in the eleventh-round as Holyfield pummeled Tyson on the ropes. Tyson showed tremendous fortitude as he refused to go down, but the referee, Mitch Halpern, stopped the contest, which will go down as one of the golden moments of boxing history.

Afterwards, Tyson himself actually added to the grand evening when he showed unexpected sportsmanship. While making his post-fight speech at the press conference podium, he called Holyfield a "great champion" and asked to embrace him because he just wanted "to touch him."

Holyfield explained the victory. "I realized Mike was going to hit me, but I knew I could take the punches.

The only thing that Mike had shown since he'd come back was he hadn't been hit."

Unfortunately, the rematch between Tyson and Holyfield would go from high to low. In the match held on June 28, 1997, Tyson twice bit a chunk off Holyfield's ear and spat it on the canvas—he was disqualified in round three.

Many observers believe Tyson purposefully cannibalized Holyfield in order to disqualify himself, rather than lose by another devastating knockout. Others say Holyfield's excessive head-butting drove Tyson over the edge. Whatever the exact truth is, Tyson's latest display of outrageous conduct would cost him a fine of $3 million as well as his license to box in Nevada.

Having disgraced himself again, Tyson was not allowed to fight with a revoked license, but he found another way to generate income—professional wrestling. Vince McMahon reportedly paid him $3 million for several wrestling show appearances in early 1998. Tyson appeared at WrestleMania XIV at the Fleet Center in Boston before 19,000 on March 29, 1998. Tyson was the "good guy/bad guy enforcer" outside the ring of the "Stone Cold" Steve Austin-Shawn Michaels WWF heavyweight title match. His role was to tease, helping Michaels all through the match. When Austin applied his "Stone Cold Stunner" maneuver, Tyson followed his cue perfectly and jumped in and pounded the three-count.

Austin then gave Tyson an "Austin 3:16" T-shirt. Michaels suddenly confronted Tyson and threw a sucker punch. Tyson blocked it and decked Michaels with his own haymaker. As the fans roared, Tyson dropped the T-shirt over the face of the supposedly unconscious

Michaels. Austin and Tyson walked out of the arena together.

Boxing greats "Marvelous" Marvin Hagler and Vinny Pazienza watched the shenanigans from ringside.

But there would be no script necessary for Tyson's next episode of violence. Months later, in the summer of 1998, he was involved in the infamous road rage incident.

Tyson's wife Monica was stopped at a light in Gaithersburg, Maryland. Tyson was in the passenger seat when their Mercedes Benz was bumped from behind by a car driven by a man named Richard Hardick, which was then bumped by Abmielec Saucedo's car. Tyson immediately jumped out and confronted both men, striking Saucedo, age sixty-two, in the face, and kicking Hardick, fifty, in the groin. The melee ended when Tyson's wife and bodyguard pulled him away.

In February of 1999, a Montgomery County judge ruled on the case, in which Tyson had pleaded no contest. Judge Stephen Johnson sentenced Tyson to two years in jail, calling it "a dramatic example, a tragic example of potentially lethal road rage." Tyson would serve a total of three months.

As Tyson's life was falling apart again, Don King and Holyfield joined forces and were calling the shots in heavyweight boxing. King, of course, had all options on Holyfield now. And he still did not fancy the idea of matching his WBA champion against the WBC champ Lennox Lewis. For nearly three years, King would protect Holyfield from a fight with Lewis.

Part of the blame rests squarely on Holyfield. He publicly expressed his desire to unify the heavyweight title on many occasions. He could have insisted that King arrange the Lewis fight. He could have told King,

"Don't worry, I'll whup Lewis." But he did not.

In December of 1997, Holyfield feigned an intent for a unification match against Lewis. He demanded the sum of $15 million. At first, no backer would agree to commit to that figure, but then, a few months later, the TV network HBO stepped up and agreed to pay Holyfield his $15 million. All was looking good — until Holyfield threw everyone for a loop by suddenly changing his tune and raising his price — to $20 million!

This bluff was astonishing from the man universally known as "The Warrior." Could it actually be that Holyfield wanted no part of a fight with Lennox Lewis? After earning more than $100 million from boxing, did Holyfield suddenly need the extra $5 million?

Whatever the motive was for playing hardball, it was far from an act of impervious confidence by Holyfield. He was beginning to look evasive about fighting Lewis. Lewis sensed Holyfield's reluctance and even began to call his rival "Evader" Holyfield.

In hindsight, after all of these events unfolded over time, it is now apparent that Tyson and Holyfield, indeed, preferred not to fight Lewis. Some staunch Lewis loyalists would even insist they were actually ducking Lewis. For many years, Lewis's reputation suffered with the public, and it was less than what it should have been. A major reason why he was regarded as the heavyweight outsider was because the American media had created and perpetuated a negative stigma against him.

Ever since the Brit first burst onto the global boxing scene in 1992, top newspaper columnists such as Ron Borges of the *Boston Globe*, Jon Saraceno of *USA Today*, Dave Anderson of *The New York Times* and Wallace Matthews, formerly of the *New York Post*, were not impressed with the fistic capabilities of Lewis. They would lace their articles about Lewis with such words and phrases as "boring," "amateurish," "clumsy and awkward," "timid," "fights scared," "lacks heart," "lethargic" and "too mild-mannered," among others. As an example of the media bias against Lewis, consider his comprehensive win over Tommy Morrison in October of 1995.

It was a dominating performance of masterful perfection over a formidable opponent. Lewis floored Morrison in round two with a left hook, a right uppercut in the fifth round, a jab in the sixth, and finally, a left hook ended the bout in the sixth. Even the bloodied and bruised Morrison offered praise to his conqueror.

"Lennox was just too good for me," confessed Morrison. "He's one helluva big guy who punches hard, and I just couldn't get past those long arms."

But the media would see the performance differently. Gerald Eskenazi of the *New York Times* concluded and wrote about Lewis, "Too bad he doesn't know how to fight."

Or how about these words from Borges in 1996 in the *Boston Globe*: "Lewis may be a professional boxer but he showed he's no fighter…most American fight fans recognize a fraud when he's in front of them, especially if he's six feet, five inches." Wallace Matthews said after another Lewis knockout victory in a title defense, "That was terrible. It looked like a Golden Gloves fight." John Rowe wrote in the *Bergen* (NJ) *Record*: "I dare you to not fall asleep watching a Lennox Lewis fight."

Fortunately, there were some experts who were more fair in their opinions. HBO's Larry Merchant was much more accurate in his assessment of Lewis. "Some fighters have a style and a personality that it takes them a long time to get recognition," Merchant said in the *Boxing Up-*

date newsletter. "They have to keep winning. Larry Holmes was a perfect example of that. It's unusual to be a Muhammad Ali or Mike Tyson, who have such an extraordinary projection of themselves as prizefighters, that people immediately respond to them."

Lewis would not be deterred. Motivated to disprove his critics and achieve his goals, he never wavered in his ambition to fight both Holyfield and Tyson or any other top threat. Actually, he would say years later that all the criticism and disrespect didn't really bother him, rather, it actually supplied him with extra incentive.

Eventually, Holyfield's pride and ego would force him into finally fighting Lewis in March of 1999. Oddsmakers made Lewis the slight 6-5 underdog. Holy-field, the class champion who was always above insulting his opposition, resorted to something he never had to do before — bold pre-fight trash talk. He promised that he would knock out Lewis in the third round. Lewis went on the verbal offensive also as he called Holyfield a "hypocrite" for preaching about his religious virtues despite having fathered numerous children out of wedlock. Lewis-Holyfield was not only a superfight, it also became a grudge match.

Lennox Lewis rose to the momentous occasion he had so long been waiting for and showed the world that he was the heavyweight master. He put on a dominating boxing display and clearly outpointed Holyfield. Punch statistics showed Lewis threw and landed approximately three times as many punches as Holyfield.

But the judges cheated Lewis. Judge Eugenia Williams scored it for Holyfield! Larry O'Connell had it as a draw! So, the match resulted in an outrageous controversial twelve-round draw! The fans booed. It was another black eye for boxing. An investigation was demanded.

Muhammad Ali even said that Lewis had been cheated.

The rematch was set for November 13, 1999. It was a tricky fight, waged cautiously by both men, but the judges got it right this time, and Lewis at long last was the undisputed Heavyweight Champion of the World. At the age of thirty-four, Lennox Lewis finally had accomplished his long and arduous mission to become the best heavyweight on the planet.

But there was still one more formidable opponent to be vanquished, one man who could complete his career and cement his legacy. Iron Mike Tyson was now the prey Lewis yearned to hunt down and destroy.

IV

"I Want To Eat Your Children!"

Speech was given to man to disguise
his thoughts.
— Charles Maurice deTalleyrand

"I'm the best ever! I'm the most brutal, vicious, ruthless heavyweight champion there's ever been. I'm Sonny Liston, I am Jack Dempsey. My style is impetuous. My defense is impregnable. I am just the most ferocious champion living today," snarled Tyson with fire in his eye, after stopping Lou Savarese in just thirty-eight seconds on June 24, 2000, in Glasgow, Scotland. Tyson had returned to boxing after the "Bite Fight" and the road rage debacle and now had three straight KO wins (over Frans Botha, Julius Francis and now Savarese, plus a no-contest against Orlin Norris, who had injured his knee).

Was Tyson finally ready to challenge the heavyweight ruler Lennox Lewis?

"Yes, Lennox Lewis, I'm coming after you," Tyson warned Showtime's interviewer Jim Grey from the ring in Glasgow. "I want to rip out your heart and feed it to you. I want to eat your children...I'm not ready for him right now. I'm rusty. I need more work. But when I'm ready, I'll destroy Lewis. When the time comes, he's no match for me. Lennox, I'm coming for you. I want your heart, I want your children, praise be to Allah."

Lennox was thousands of miles away from Tyson when he heard those words. He was in the final stages of training in the eastern Pennsylvania mountains for his July 15 defense against Frans Botha. When asked about Tyson's threats, he smiled as if it was all just silliness.

"Hearing the statement that Tyson wants to eat my heart and eat my children kind of confuses me," Lewis said during a midweek open media workout at his training camp. "Because I thought he was a vegetarian. It was simply a preposterous statement. But before he has a chance to eat me, Tyson has to eat my left and right crosses. And he knows what he can have for dessert."

Lewis, the undisputed heavyweight champion of the planet, was unimpressed by Tyson's win over Savarese, whose name the champion intentionally mispronounced as *Savar-easy*.

"I had seen Savarese against Michael Grant, and he was in better shape. Against Tyson he had a potbelly, and he didn't seem like he was there to win. 'Savareasy' seemed like he was there to catch a quality punch, take his money ($850,000) and go home."

Of course, Tyson managed to get himself in trouble yet again. As Refereee John Coyle was halting the bout, Tyson leapt in over Coyle to land more blows; one even struck the referee. Tyson was later fined $187,000 for the late hits on Savarese.

Coyle said, "I didn't take a full shot. I think, if I had, I'd still be in the hospital. Tyson just wanted to keep fighting after he won the fight. It was the first time I had ever had that. It was quite strange."

Former WBA Featherweight Champion Barry McGuigan of Ireland was horrified by Tyson's antics.

"What he did was appalling," said McGuigan in *Boxing Update* newsletter. "He showed complete con-tempt for authority. Tyson is clearly out of control out of the ring. And out of control in it."

James Watt, the former WBC Lightweight Champion from Glasgow, Scotland, was also disgusted. "The man is not a sportsman. He's a devil. He has shamed boxing once again. Las Vegas doesn't want him. And we don't want him, either."

Scottish National Party Leader Alex Salmond said in *Boxing Update* newsletter, "The so-called economic benefits of which Jack Straw [British Home Secretary] based his disgraceful decision to let convicted rapist Mike Tyson into Scotland proved to be totally illusory. Women's groups and Scottish Parliament were absolutely right to oppose the so-called fight. It would have been far better all around if it had never taken place."

Emanuel Steward, as usual, had a perceptive take on Tyson and his growing discontent about discussing all things pertaining to Lennox Lewis.

"I believe Mike Tyson is actually afraid of Lennox, and I think Lennox is a big thorn in Tyson's side," Steward surmised. "I think it's driving Tyson crazy. If they clash, I think it will be a quick evening. I can see a one-round KO victory for Lewis."

To reinforce his point, Steward reminded his listeners of the psychological importance of the step-aside payment from Tyson to avoid boxing Lewis in 1996. That was an ineradicable act by Tyson that awarded not only cash but also a distinct mental edge to Lewis. In the mental warfare between Lewis and Tyson, this fact was hugely significant.

"Tyson paid four million dollars not to fight Lennox. And when Lennox said he didn't want any step-aside money, that he just wanted to fight for Tyson's title, Tyson still didn't want to fight him. What does that tell you? But forget about Tyson. He may never fight Lennox. Because he's scared to death of him. That's why he talks so much. I learned a long time ago that real tough guys don't talk tough. They don't have to."

The Lewis-Botha fight in London was of paramount importance. The eyes and ears of the world were on Lewis now, judging how he would respond to Tyson's verbal offensive three weeks earlier in Glasgow. Also, it was the first fight in his homeland since the McCall defeat.

But Lewis would produce magnificently under the pressure. In possibly the most spectacular win of his career—as Ali's finest performance is widely considered his 1966 KO over Cleveland Williams—Lewis annihilated Botha in the second round with a pinpoint-accurate four-punch combination. To make it an even more perfect evening, Lewis landed the winning punches just moments after the 10,000-strong London Arena crowd had begun chanting "Lewis! Lewis!" No man had ever decimated Botha with such ease and dominance. Not even Tyson, who struggled to a fifth-round KO in 1999 after being surprisingly outboxed by "The White Buffalo."

In the interview afterward, with HBO's Larry Merchant, Lewis addressed Tyson.

"Put up or shut up! Sign the contract tomorrow," he demanded. "He's been talking about what he can eat.

[He held up his right fist.] I'll show him what he can eat."

Lewis had more to say. "Let's get it on now. Stop the mad talk. I'm into reality. Let's step in the ring...I'm going to definitely be the guy that puts him to sleep...In one sense, I look at myself as a savior for boxing, by getting rid of all the misfits. You could say that Mike Tyson is the last misfit of boxing.

"You know, Tyson's like a mascot, in a way. The people want to see *Who is this guy who beats up old people on the street, and bites people?* He's like a train wreck waiting to happen. So, people are always excited to see a train wreck, plane crash or anything like that."

Tyson's anticipated rebuttal in this war of words never came—he would not be seen or heard from for weeks. His advisor, Shelly Finkel, was asked Tyson's assessment of the Lewis-Botha fight as well as his reply to Lewis's challenge. Finkel claimed Tyson was home in Phoenix and did not watch the fight on television. Yeah, right.

Though Lewis was obligated to defend next against IBF number-one-ranked mandatory challenger David Tua by November, the preference was to fight Tyson.

"I am willing to sidestep Tua and box Tyson straight away," Lewis made clear. "I would get a lot of money to fight Tyson. But the main reason for getting in the ring would be to knock him out. Tyson's style cannot beat me."

The main obstacle in making Lewis-Tyson, aside from Tyson's hesitance, was the TV network dilemma. Lewis was under contract exclusively to HBO, and Tyson to Showtime. Seth Abraham, then the head of Time Warner Sports, the parent company of HBO, said,

"We've got the heavyweight champion, they've got the challenger. We'll figure it out."

Tyson seemed in no mood to even begin negotiations for a Lewis fight. In fact, there were whispers and hints he might retire from boxing.

"That's hard to say. Maybe the other day when Mike said [he was considering retirement], he meant it," Finkel said. "But that could change in a couple of days."

This was another evasion by Tyson regarding a match with Lewis. Was Tyson actually tiring of the boxing game and of earning about $10 million per fight? Or was he perhaps a little too much in secret admiration of Lennox Lewis—remember, Tyson is a great student of the game, and he surely knows a great fighter when he sees one. Did Tyson know better than anybody that Lewis was truly the man possessing the brains and brawn to knock him out once and for all?

Tyson re-emerged from his silent retreat to fight Andrew Golota in October of 2000 in Detroit. But Mike's time away from the ring was hardly a healthy and rejuvenating respite. It was just more scandalous, troublesome and overindulgent behavior. Already, in February, Tyson settled a claim of assault lodged by two Washington DC women. In May, he was accused but not charged with assaulting a topless dancer at a club called Cheetah's in Las Vegas. In July, he was accused but not charged with sexually assaulting a California woman. There were also rumors that Tyson was videotaping his meetings with prostitutes, so as to avoid any potential rape allegations.

Then there were rumored leaks to the media that Tyson had a violent disagreement with British promoter Frank Warren after his January KO win over Julius Francis. The dispute was over a balance of $690,000 due on a jewelry purchase reportedly made by Tyson. Warren, who promoted Tyson-Francis in Manchester, England, denied Tyson's insistence he was obligated to pay the balance. The two apparently had a physical altercation at the Grosvenor Hotel in Glasgow, just days before the Savarese fight. For his temerity, Warren suffered facial bruises, a left eye that was bloodshot and sore ribs. Rumors even swirled that Tyson almost hurled Warren out of the seventh-floor hotel window. According to the *London Sun*, Warren was ready to file criminal assault charges against Tyson, which in all likelihood, would have put Tyson back in jail for a third time—and perhaps even ended his career.

Tyson was in the dressing room getting ready for Savarese when he finally verbally agreed to pay Warren the sum of $3,000,000 not to take criminal action. Before he headed to the ring, he reluctantly had to take off his gloves to sign a new contract for Warren—Warren was ensuring he would be paid. No Tyson verbal promises would suffice.

Despite the brewing troubles constantly surrounding Tyson, his trainer Tommy Brooks was singing praises of how good Tyson looked in training. You would have thought that Cus and Kevin Rooney were still around.

"Mike Tyson is better now than he was, even before incarceration. He is looking sensational in the gym. The people are going to see the Tyson of old." Brooks claimed in *Boxing Update*. "Lennox is a super-nice person, but in the ring he is too laid back. I think Lennox needs more belief in himself. He hasn't got enough firepower, and that's gonna be the burning issue when Mike fights him.

"That is what Mike will expose and take advantage of. Mike isn't worried who he fights. He can beat whoever he fights. Mike will be back on top again, it's just a matter of time."

Trainer Jesse Reid spent about ten days working with Tyson but decided not to stick around. He offered a more objective perspective of the situation.

"Tyson has no one he can really respect, and he listens to no one," Reid revealed to *Boxing Update*. "Tommy Brooks has had Tyson for three fights now. He's a nice guy but I feel sorry for him. When the bell rings, Tyson is going to fight exactly the way he wants to. Whether Tyson is right or wrong, everybody who has ever been around him just says Yes, yes, yes."

Before the Golota fight, Tyson revealed his bizarre state of mind with some perplexing statements to the media.

"I'm on the Zoloft thing," he said. "But I'm on that to keep me from killing y'all...I don't care about living or dying. I'm a dysfunctional motherfucker!...Look at me. I've been embarrassed. Humiliation. Degradation. And any other [word that ends in] t-i-o-n that you can think of...I'm in pain."

He may have been suffering from severe mental anguish, but Tyson proved he could still put it all together to do what he does best—fight. Against Golota, he won the first round with a vintage overhand right that floored Golota heavily. But the talented Golota survived that knockdown and a nasty cut from a head-butt, and even seemed to outbox Tyson in the second round. The match was beginning to get interesting.

Then, unexpectedly, Golota refused to answer the bell for the third round, infuriating his trainers. He just quit. Once again, Tyson looked confused in victory.

It was to be yet another controversial event involving Tyson. After the fight, he refused to take a drug test, and because of that, the outcome was eventually changed to a "no contest" by the Michigan State Athletic Commission.

Tyson's latest performance was of little benefit as a tune-up fight for the anticipated, eventual showdown with Lewis, who had previously obliterated Golota in one round back in 1997. Interestingly, ten days after the Golota fight, Tyson decided to pay an uninvited visit to see Lewis, who was in training for his upcoming November 11 title defense against Tua.

Lewis left the Poconos for a day to do a public workout/press conference inside Grand Central Terminal's Vanderbilt Hall in New York City on October 31. To everyone's surprise, Tyson appeared and quietly watched Lewis shadowbox for a few moments without incident. But Tyson had to quickly exit because of the commotion his presence caused. Was he making an attempt to somehow intimidate his nemesis? Or was he paying homage to the undisputed champion? It was hard to tell.

One thing was for sure—Lewis would have his hands full with the twenty-seven-year-old bull named Tua. The insiders' opinion was that the hard-punching Samoan was a very dangerous threat to Lewis. At five feet, ten inches, two hundred-forty-five pounds, Tua was similar in stature to Tyson but even wider and thicker. Tua—whose birth name was Mafaufau Tavito Lio Mafaufau Sanerivi Talimatasi—sported a fine record of 37-1-0 with 32 KOs. The one defeat was a very close, controversial decision to the unbeaten Nigerian Ike Ibeabuchi in 1997.[4]

Tua's strategy to dethrone Lewis was simple.

"I have the style to knock out Lennox Lewis," Tua

---

[4] Ibeabuchi is the former prospect currently incarcerated in Nevada after a disastrous encounter with a call girl.

declared at the press conference. "He's six-five. I feel my height at five-ten is a big advantage for me. Lewis has looked good with bigger and taller guys. As for me, he would have to punch down. Being shorter, I'm in a position to attack Lewis' body. Michael Grant was a safer fight because he was right there for Lennox's right hand. For many years, Lewis has looked good facing tall guys because all he had to do is punch at them. With me, he'll be in with a guy that can slip punches and who will be hitting him in the body and in the chest. Lennox is tailor-made for me."

Many experts figured that this was a battle-plan that could topple Lewis. At the least, it would be a gauge of how Tyson would fare with Lewis. Even Tyson himself expressed support for Tua's chances.

"Tua is dangerously underestimated," Tyson said in *Boxing Update*. "We have been looking at him for a year, and he has plenty of guts and the ability to seriously threaten Lewis. Forget Botha. He's not even a contender for the title. But Tua could be. He is angry, mean and hungry. Tua has that look in his eye. Like he's ready to kill someone. I hope it's not Lewis, because I want to end Lewis."

Tyson's worries of Tua demolishing Lewis would prove to be baseless. Lewis was masterful in completely dominating Tua. It was a classical performance by a pugilist specialist on the art of hit and not get hit. Like a matador completely taming a wild, raging bull, it was the science of boxing at its brilliant best. It was such a comprehensive unanimous decision that Tyson and his handlers had to be glum-faced watching it. No boxer had ever so dominated the very dangerous Tua.

But after the fine win over Tua, overconfidence and complacence seemed to plague the undisputed heavyweight champion again. He was getting tired of waiting and waiting for Tyson to step up. He would make some poor decisions before his next fight, scheduled in April 2001 against twenty-eight-year-old journeyman contender Hasim Rahman. First, he set his training camp — for the first time — in Las Vegas. This was to enable him to make a cameo appearance in the blockbuster Julia Roberts/George Clooney/Brad Pitt/Matt Damon film *Ocean's Eleven*.

But the filming schedule would be delayed; and Lewis paid the price, as he was unable to get to South Africa until fewer than ten full days before the fight. This misfortune raised many eyebrows, because it was not nearly enough time for Lennox to acclimatize. The champion arrived to the strange new continent he had never visited before looking fit but heavier than his norm.[5]

I was told by a camp member Lewis went to jog one day and "he had to stop after one mile." The 5,500-ft.-above-sea-level altitude was severely affecting his breathing.

Meanwhile, Rahman had arrived in South Africa nearly a month before the fight date. The locals embraced "The Rock" and his amiable, down-to-earth and pleasant nature. Unexpectedly, the 6-1 underdog challenger became the sentimental favorite. Lewis was respected as the champion, but the likable and gregarious Rahman had won the hearts of many of the South Africans.

The warning signs were all there for the possible upset. Rahman's state of mind and biorhythms appeared to

---

[5] Lewis would weigh in at 253, the heaviest of his career.

be excellent. He was in optimum condition. And Rock was aware that Lewis was not.

The plan was to force Lewis into the later rounds. Lewis, it seemed, expected to dispose of the far less accomplished Rahman without much struggle. Rah-man's ability to take a punch was questionable because Tua and Oleg Maskaev had previously knocked him out.

South African Corrie Sanders also had Rahman in big trouble.

Still, Lewis was winning the fight. But the champion's form was not nearly as sharp or up to the standards we had come to expect. He was breathing heavily early on, and his footwork was sloppy and laborious. Rahman eventually began to land big punches. In the fifth round, he jolted Lewis with a big right, which elicited a smile.

Rock ignored the bluff. He sensed his foe was vulnerable now and went for the kill. About a minute later, he had Lewis on the ropes. Lewis again smiled, but Rahman smelled victory. He loaded up and launched a perfect home-run overhand right that landed right on the button. The champion went down heavily on his back.

Somehow, he managed to get up, but the referee signaled it was all over. Just like that, the World Heavyweight title changed hands.

Fortunately for Lewis, he and his business manager Adrian Ogun had had the sense to insert a rematch clause into the fight contract. Perhaps it was some kind of premonition, because this was not typical Lewis contract procedure. Not surprising, the new champion Rahman did not want to honor it. As it turned out, he was lured away from his former promoter Cedric Kushner by none other than Don King—and a suitcase containing a reported $200,000 cash.

King promised Rahman easy money fights with Brian Nielsen and David Izon for $20 million. Lewis could not let this happen or else his career — and aspirations of conquering Tyson — would be finished. Once again, Team Lewis had to take an opponent to court in order to get them into the ring.

Manhattan Federal Court Judge Miriam Cederbaum eventually ruled Rahman must either honor the rematch clause and fight Lewis — or not fight at all for the next eighteen months. Cederbaum said Lewis would be irreparably harmed if he were not granted the rematch. She believed evidence offered in the two-week trial, conducted without a jury, demonstrated that the thirty-five-year-old Lewis could likely fight only two more years.

"And even in the next two years," Judge Cederbaum concluded, "his powers as a fighter will be diminishing."

Wladimir Klitschko, then an outstanding heavyweight prospect and currently the IBF/WBO heavyweight champion, was also involved in the *Ocean's Eleven* movie with Lewis. Klitschko performed in the boxing scene as Lewis's fictional opponent. Klitschko spent time with Lewis and got to know him. The Ukrainian believes complacence cost Lewis his championship.

"Lewis said to me, If I don't knock that guy out in five rounds, I should retire," he recalled. "But I thought his mental attitude was not good. He completely underestimated Rahman. He talked more about the film and even fighting me someday down the road than he did about Rahman. I just never had the feeling he was taking it seriously. For the rematch, I'm sure he will."

The rematch was set for November 17, 2001, at Mandalay Bay in Las Vegas. This time Lewis had no distractions such as movie star roles with Julia Roberts. And he was back in his favorite training environment, the Caesars Brookdale Resort in the Pocono Mountains of eastern Pennsylvania. Lewis said if he were to lose to Rahman again there would be no sense in fighting on. It was either win or retire. His career legacy and a big-money fight with Tyson hung in the balance.

Rahman sought to get under Lewis's skin on their press tour by questioning his sexuality on several occasions. Lewis, who had made it known he would not marry until after his boxing career was finished, could not ignore the disrespect from Rahman. After two days of Rahman's jibes, egos collided into a full-scale brawl at the ESPN studio where the two fighters were doing an interview with Gary Miller for the television show *Up Close*.

At first, it was Rahman who seemed to win the confrontation as he wrestled Lewis onto his back after the studio table broke. Lewis got up, though, and had to be restrained from getting back at Rahman, who appeared to backpedal away from the infuriated Lewis.

Meanwhile, Tyson was inactive during this entire period until he stopped a pudgy and mismatched Brian Nielsen in seven rounds in Copenhagen, Denmark, on October 13, 2001. It was another long layoff—348 days—for him. Though he looked good at times, once again throwing his signature bombs in combinations, the game Nielsen did not put up much of a fight. He seemed more like a durable heavy bag than a competitive opponent.

Showtime Network's ratings for the fight, which was shown in the US on tape delay, were disappointing. Fans were getting tired of watching Tyson in meaningless fights. Showtime was losing patience, too. Time was running out for Tyson. He would have to fight in a more attractive match-up for his next fight.

Tyson was apparently disinterested, too. Against Nielsen, he weighed in at 239, which was sixteen pounds heavier than his previous high.

The Lewis-Rahman contest was much more intriguing. The combatants had developed a seething dislike for each other. They even had to be kept apart by a steel barricade at the weigh-in. Rahman was confident—probably overconfident—as he carried on like a young Cassius Clay at the press conference. Lewis was subdued, even "disengaged" from all the hoopla, as TV commentator Max Kellerman put it. But the lion was waiting for the moment to exact revenge.

On fight night, it was Lewis who was the commander-in-chief. He emerged from his dressing room in a white, Grim Reaper-like hood with a trance-like expression on his face as his ring entry musical choice of James Brown's "The Big Payback" played in the background. Like an assassin, he looked more than ready to do what he had to do.

The totally focused look in his eyes that night had to have some effect on Rahman, who was surely watching the television monitor in his dressing room. When he appeared moments later, he looked agitated, as if he saw something in those eyes that he didn't expect. As if, all of a sudden, he realized his foolish error in making all those disrespectful insults to Lewis had given his opponent extra incentive.

Lewis came up with one of the greatest performances of his career. It was a defining moment for his legacy. A single, perfect right hand ended the fight in the fourth round. It was one of the most aesthetically awesome knockouts ever seen in a ring, comparable with Ali-Foreman, Marciano-Walcott, Tyson-Berbick, Louis-

Schmeling. Lewis's punch struck loudly off Rahman's jaw.

Now, finally, the time had come. A Lewis vs. Tyson heavyweight title match could be made, at last. The winding marathon process had played itself out. The near-decade-long undertaking was almost over. The moment of truth was almost a reality.

Little did we all know that the wildest part of the adventure was still to come.

V

Horror At The Hudson Theatre

> Silence alone is great. All else is
> weakness.
>
> — DeVigny

The fight was coming.

Vigorous negotiations between the Lewis and Tyson
camps and the television networks took place over the
holidays at the end of 2001. The complicated dealings
were so tenuous that HBO pay-per-view executive Mark
Taffet jokingly told me I could write a book on just those
negotiations alone.

When all the parties were at last somewhat satisfied
with their pieces of the pie, the media was notified that
January 22 was the date of the official press conference
to announce that Lewis-Tyson would actually be con-
tested on April 6 in Las Vegas.

Upon learning of this long-awaited news, many
members of the press harbored mixed feelings of surprise, curiosity and excitement. On the one hand, the
Super Fight, a decade in the making, was at last on the

verge. It would be such an important and electrifying event for the sport. But there was still the underlying suspicion that Tyson was being forced into this fight more because of financial pressures than because he truly wanted it for competitive reasons. This spelled trouble.

Because putting the unreliable and volatile Tyson into such a high-pressure situation as fighting for the world heavyweight title was a risky idea in the first place. There were many insiders who openly wondered if Tyson was even fit to function in society, let alone fight for the most prestigious and respected prize in sport. Millions of dollars were going to be invested to make this mega-event happen. Another Tyson explosion could ruin everything. Just asking him to cooperate with such a small matter as the media obligations could be dangerous. Everyone knew the rumors floating around that he was said to be broke, unhappy and, on top of that, rejected by his wife. Monica Tyson had filed for divorce on January 5.

But the show would have to go on. It must go on. The jackpot for a Lewis-Tyson match would be colossal. It had the potential to be the biggest prizefight in history.

There was a definite aura of tension at high noon in the Hudson Theatre inside the Millenium Hotel at W. 44th Street near Times Square in Manhattan.

"Immediately when I walked in the place, I detected something could happen," WBC President Jose Sulaiman would say after. An hour later, he would be knocked unconscious and then taken to a hospital.

Before the official proceedings even began that day, a bizarre tone was established. I've seen many boxing press conferences turn into circuses, but this one took the cake. The opening act was Tyson's official cheerleader, a man in his forties better known as "Crocodile." Outfitted in army fatigues, shades and a matching camouflage Gilligan-type fishing hat, Crocodile—Steve Fitch is his real name—hollered for twenty minutes his redundant sound bites of "Guerilla warfare!" and "Mike will *destroy* Lennox, *guaranteed!*"

The journalists sitting in the press rows of the theatre were enjoying every minute of it. *New York Post* columnist Wally Matthews wondered aloud, "What does he put on his tax return for 'occupation?'" Dave Anderson, the Pulitzer Prize-winner from *The New York Times* remarked, "This sure isn't like covering The Masters."

The show got better as it went along. Suddenly, a mountainous black man in a stylish, shiny-gold paisley suit topped off, for some unknown reason, by a Phantom of the Opera-style mask began bellowing and waving his arms from the balcony behind and above us. It was Mitchell Rose, the one-time journeyman Brooklyn heavyweight with a 2-7-1 record, best-known as the first man to KO Butterbean.

Rose, now an auto body shop and liquor store owner, had had a brawl with Tyson at the Sugar Hill nightclub in the wee hours of a Sunday morning the previous December. And Rose was there to inform Tyson that he had to pay for the $5,000 mink coat Mike had "tore up like it was paper."

Rose was not there to make discreet inquiries. Instead he was roaring from the balcony, "No one's makin' any money until my coat's paid for. That motherfucker Tyson is a homo who touched my ass in the club and smoked blunts [marijuana joints] all night long. Now he's losing his wife over messin' with those chicken heads [ghetto slang for promiscuous girls]!" Rose's loud monologue went on for a good minute.

After Rose completed his statement, he suddenly pulled out a plastic bag of what appeared to be either marijuana or oregano. The former heavyweight boxer tossed the contents into the air from the balcony, and we all watched it fall down on us. Main Events promoter Kathy Duva tried to shake the substance out of her hair.

Just try to imagine this scene of chaos. This was the mood, this was the atmosphere before Lewis or Tyson even appeared.

A few moments later, they emerged. Suddenly, the lights dimmed, and a Tyson action video was played on a large movie screen. From the right side of the stage, out strutted the man himself—Iron Mike Tyson. Then the Lewis video, and from the left side strode the cool, undisputed heavyweight champion. There they stood, facing each other. Finally, after all those years of waiting, there was Mike Tyson and Lennox Lewis, face to face.

The instrumental music was blaring. Everyone watched in frozen awe as Tyson and Lewis looked at each other, about twenty feet apart. Lewis had on a light gray suit, a ragamuffin-type hat and shades. Tyson was wearing all black and a backwards black beret. Suddenly, and unexpectedly, Tyson charged Lewis, and it didn't appear like he was intending to shake hands.

For some reason, Tyson removed and tossed away his hat on the way over toward Lewis. A bodyguard of the champion named Troy Muhammad alertly rushed out from stage left. Instantaneously, Tyson greeted Muhammad with his left fist, though Iron Mike's sneak punch missed the bodyguard by a good ten inches at least. He may have intended to miss—that's the way it looked to my eyes.

But Lewis was not about to wait for Tyson's next

sucker punch. Instead, he clobbered Tyson with a chopping right.

At that point, all hell broke loose—punches, fists, shoving, flying objects, it was a live riot twenty yards away. Everyone in the audience was on their feet now. Was this really happening?

This was certainly not a staged brawl to generate extra publicity. This was real.

"Shelly Finkel called me last night," said Lewis promoter Gary Shaw after it was all over. "He told me nothing's going to happen. Mike just wants to stare him down. So, we had two podiums set up. I went back to talk to Lennox. Lennox said, Fine, if he wants to have a face-off, I'll have a face-off."

"I have no doubt he was definitely trying to sucker punch me," Lewis would say later. "Rushing across the stage, throwing down the hat...I have no doubt he was planning something. And I wasn't going to wait around to find out."

When the mayhem finally did quell, though not until after about two or three minutes, Tyson emerged to the front right of the stage with his arms aloft in triumph, acting as if he'd just won something. Nobody knew— maybe he had beaten Lewis unconscious. Lewis was still not in view. Was he injured? Where was he?[6]

Then Tyson began grabbing his crotch and making obscene gestures to the Lewis section sitting in the audience. That group, which included the champ's mother Violet, was sitting in the front left rows. This is when I cupped my hands and loudly booed Tyson.

Everyone in the place heard me, including Tyson, who was momentarily stunned. He quickly identified

---

[6] Lewis was okay, except for a bite on his thigh from Tyson.

his heckler in the sixth row, and he looked very pissed off. I didn't care that he saw me boo him. I was angry, too. This man had just committed three crimes—first-degree assault on the world heavyweight champion, lewd behavior and disturbing the peace. And nobody else was saying or doing a damn thing about it. Where the hell were the police? We'd just watched a criminal break the law and then raise his arms in victory.

When Tyson and I made eye contact, he tried to intimidate me, but for some reason, I wasn't scared. I was still far more disgusted by his crime spree than worried about any dirty looks.

Tyson was still standing there surrounded by his entourage, which included boxer Zab Judah and trainer Stacey McKinley and a few others. He turned away from the audience, thinking his heckler was finished. But I wasn't. About thirty seconds later, without considering the consequences, I cupped my hands to my mouth again. This time I shouted "Get him a straitjacket!"

Tyson erupted like it was the first time in a very long time anyone had insulted him to his face, in front of a crowd. He knew who had made the heckle and would not tolerate any more of my disrespect. He took a few threatening steps to the lip of the stage and launched into a vicious tirade. This is what Tyson said to me:

"Fuck you, you ho! Come and say it to my face up here, whiteboy! I'll (inaudible) your ass in front of everybody! You bitch. Come on, you punk-ass bitch! You're scared, coward! See, you're scared! You're not man enough to fuck with me!…You can't touch me! You're not man enough! I'll eat your (inaudible) alive, motherfucker! You can't last two minutes in my world, bitch! Look at you, you're scared now, you ho! Scared like a little white pussy! Scared of the real man! I'll fuck you till you love me, faggot!"

I tried to maintain a stoic expression despite the vulgarity of the verbal assault. For a few seconds, I felt fear, Holy shit! Tyson might actually come down and decapitate me. But for the most part I stood there calmly, never breaking eye contact with him. For some reason, I just sensed that he wouldn't physically assault me because, deep down, he knew I was right and everybody else knew it, too.

If either one of us blinked first, it was Mike Tyson. It even seemed, at one point, like my colleague Joe Cichelli of *Boxing World* magazine observed, he was crying underneath the rage.

As the rant wore on, it lost power. Tyson, who deep down is a goodhearted man and can be a gentleman, seemed to be coming back to his senses. He kept looking at me, as if to make sure I would shout nothing else. Eventually, he slowly turned away and blended in with his cohorts. His crew patted his back for comfort, consoling him as if he was the one who had been wounded.

For me, it was time to get the hell out of there. I didn't want to risk someone coming up from behind and planting a sucker punch on me. So they could go back and tell Mike how they got that punk. I picked up my things, said a few hasty goodbyes and made myself scarce.

I didn't miss much, though I was informed later that Tyson was seen smiling in the street signing autographs and taking pictures with fans. As if nothing had happened.

Later that day, Tyson would explain his actions in a statement.

"I came to New York to promote a fight that I want

and boxing fans came to see. I am not a role model or Mr. Politically Correct."

Clinical psychologist Dr. Jeffrey Gardere had a different opinion, after he evaluated a videotape of the press conference rampage.

"We see from his psychiatric history and, of course, his boxing history that he has poor impulse control, to put it very mildly," Dr. Gardere said on a network newscast interview. "I believe that was a situation where, as soon as he thought in his mind his machoism was being challenged, then he was not able to control himself.

"I think that Mike Tyson is a person that perhaps needs to be separated from boxing for some time in order for him to get help, some good therapeutic help. Probably including some sort of psychiatric medications in addition to the psychotherapy. He needs to have some sort of life coach. If he doesn't get the proper help, he's going to self-destruct. He might end up doing something even crazier than biting other people. He might end up, at some point, killing himself."

Tyson's former assistant trainer from his teen years, Teddy Atlas, had another view. "He might be trying to sabotage the fight," Atlas speculated in *Boxing Update*. "Everybody's afraid. It's just a matter of being able to control it.

"I think the way for Tyson to control it is with confidence, with discipline, with living the right way. When you start living the wrong way, when you don't have discipline in your life, it's very hard to get ready and go inside that ring and feel like a warrior. I think Tyson is having trouble from keeping the wolves from the door right now. There's a lot of self-doubt that's creeping in there.

"I'm not saying he's not going to fight. I'm just saying he's not sure of himself. And when you're not sure of yourself, you do things to sabotage yourself. And you do things to make the fight easier. And you try to intimidate the guy so you don't have to go in there and face the guy on an even playing field. Because you don't believe you can."

Oscar De La Hoya was outraged at Tyson. "He's a circus act and he's killing boxing. He's disgusting. It's sad and depressing. There are so many good boxers, and he ruins it for everyone. I love this sport, but I hate what's happening. A lot of young fighters try to imitate the guys at the top. And he's the worst role model in the world. I don't think he's acting anymore. I think he's seriously sick."

Promoter Bob Arum was also horrified by Tyson's role at the press conference. "Mike Tyson is the biggest disgrace in the history of boxing. There's never been an insane fighter at the top of boxing. He should be locked up in an insane asylum instead of having people pay to see him."

Now the fight, and the potential $100 million in profits, were in serious jeopardy. Tyson's license to fight in Las Vegas was pending a hearing the following week before the Nevada State Athletic Commission. Boxers must renew their license every year. Tyson's license had been revoked in 1997 after the ear-biting incident and had been "cautiously reinstated" the following year. At that hearing, one of the commissioners asked Tyson's lawyer Jim Jimmerson, "Is there anything that's going to come back and haunt [our awarding Tyson his reinstatement]?" Jimmerson assured him, "The answer is clearly no. Mr. Tyson will make you proud." Jim Jimmerson is still eating those words.

The impact the Lewis-Tyson fight would have had on

Las Vegas was staggering. For major fights, the Las Vegas Convention and Visitor's Authority estimates the windfall for hotels, retailers and restaurants to be around $8-12 million. Overall, Las Vegas stood to profit an estimated $300 million the weekend of the fight.

But Mayor pro tem Gary Reese didn't care much about that fact. "This fight isn't make or break for this city. If they can't act like gentleman in a dress rehearsal, we don't need them. The city of Las Vegas needs to be protected. We are a resort destination for a lot of people. Everybody who I've been in contact with says we don't need it."

But the hotels needed it. Tourism in Las Vegas was down following the 9/11 tragedy. Hotel rates and occupancies were slow to recover. And for major boxing events, casinos invite hundreds, sometimes thousands of high-rolling gamblers to watch. Fight fans fly into Vegas from around the globe. The MGM Grand was expecting a sellout crowd of 17,157.

"This fight could have a far greater impact than any fight before it," said Scott Ghertner, director of sports and promotions for MGM Mirage, the hotel's parent company. "And it would definitely help the city return to what we were before Nine-eleven."

When Tyson appeared before the commission on January 29, the panel made it clear they were more disturbed by his horrid rant *after* the brawl with Lewis. They asked Mike, "Do you have any friends that you can talk to?"

Tyson answered, "I don't have one friend in my entire life. My experience in life produced the person that I am. And the person that I am has never been successful with friends."

Mike asked for leniency. "I'm not Mother Teresa. And

I'm not Charles Manson, either," he pleaded. "I could assure you on my behalf, on behalf of my conduct as a gentleman of the sport, you will never see that behavior happen from me again. My interests weren't to hurt no one or to inflict pain on the champion or anybody else associated with him."

But the commission was not impressed. They had heard it all before. The vote was 4-1 rejecting Tyson's application for license.[7]

John Bailey, one of the commissioners, told Tyson, "I believe you tarnished and diminished the profession and the sport. It seems to me that you took your relicensing by this commission for granted." Another commissioner Amy Ayoub said, "We will not tolerate this kind of behavior from Mr. Tyson, not in boxing, not in Nevada. To relicense you sends the message that uncontrollable, violent behavior gets rewarded with multi-million dollar paydays. I can't send that message. There comes a time when you have to start taking responsibilty for your actions."

Tyson was typically repugnant in accepting the decision. He called Lewis a "coward" and added, "I'll fight him any time I see him on the street."

Despite the fact that Las Vegas had slammed the door in the face of Tyson, the fight was still expected to take place eventually. As Bob Ley said on an ESPN special, "The last five days have been the greatest commercial in the world for the fight."

This was true, as all the major TV networks in America and around the world over and over aired video clips

---

[7] Note: The commission did not ask Tyson about a sexual assault allegation he was facing in Las Vegas. But ten days later, the Clark County district attorney decided not to indict Tyson, even though they had earlier collected evidence which supported the accusation.

of the brawl and the Tyson tirade. The coverage went on for days. It was front page news all over the world. Virtually everybody in the media—like Bill O'Reilly, Larry King, Dan Rather, Peter Jennings, Tom Brokaw, Sean Hannity and most of the major newspaper columnists—were all commenting on the issue of Tyson and Lewis. Major newspapers ran screaming front page headlines like "Mad Mike," "Raging Mike," "Re-Pug-Nant," "Cannibal."

Fox News's Bill O'Reilly, host of the hugely popular *The O'Reilly Factor* said on-air, "I just think this is a sad reflection of America today. I think Tyson's a thug, and he rapes women and he's a brutal guy. I don't care that he throws around money. I think it's sad that America allows this kind of stuff to happen. HBO and Showtime should be ashamed of themselves for sponsoring this."

But nobody was about to give up on making the fight a reality. There was too much money to be made. Promoters worked diligently to find a new venue for the fight, one that would license Tyson.

Emanuel Steward was confident the fight would happen. "I definitely feel the fight will happen for two reasons," Lewis's trainer said. "As bad and appalling as what Tyson did was, the public wants to see the fight. And Lennox wants a piece of Tyson very badly. The public has no idea how much Lennox wants this fight."

VI

Memphis Or Bust

When money speaks, the truth keeps
silent.
— Russian proverb

New Jersey, Los Angeles, Miami, Houston, Germany,
Italy, Indonesia, South Africa, Colorado, Egypt, Detroit,
South Korea, Beirut, Washington DC...

Every few days there were new rumors about new
host sites for Lewis-Tyson. Localities around the globe
aspired to lure the mammoth boxing event, which was
now open to bid. For a time, it looked as if Lewis and
Tyson would be headed to the MCI Center in Washington DC; the DC Boxing Commission agreed to license
Tyson on March 12. This was considered a major step, as
attempts to get Tyson licenses in Texas and Georgia had
failed. Another earlier potential site was Colorado, but
those talks fizzled.

March 15 was the date the original Lewis-Tyson contract set as the deadline. Otherwise, if a contract and fight venue had not been finalized, Lewis had the option to pull out of the original contract and demand fundamental changes or even pull out of the fight altogether. When DC got seriously involved, Lewis agreed to extend the expiration date ten days to allow negotiations to continue, but the money that local Washington DC officials boasted of to fund the fight never materialized.

That's when Brian Young, a thirty-five-year-old enterprising boxing promoter from Nashville, Tennessee, got the process started. I met Brian in June of 2007 at Madison Square Garden, where he was co-promoting Zab Judah against Miguel Angel Cotto for Cotto's WBA Welterweight title. He explained in fascinating detail how he, as a small local promoter, was able to play a major role in producing one of the biggest fights in boxing history.

"Let me first say how much I appreciate you taking the time out to write a book about Lewis-Tyson," said Young. "It was certainly a special event that impacted a considerable amount of lives. That time period was the most exciting of my life, and I will never forget them. There were a lot of hurdles that kept arising, but I truly believe it was a blessing from God that the fight was meant to happen, and we kept pressing until it became a reality."

"The first idea I had about promoting Lewis-Tyson was when I was working at Hermitage Fitness Center in East Nashville. I was working there forty hours a week in addition to promoting our shows in Nashville and at the Mississippi casinos. Tyson's license was denied January ninth in Las Vegas, I believe, and a few days later it hit me that with my connections at the state level and in boxing circles I could see myself being able to put everybody together. Nothing against working at the fitness center, but it wasn't really where my heart was, which explains why my mind was working overtime while I was on the clock there as to how I could create a break for us and just be able to do boxing fulltime.

"I was reading where Detroit, Dallas and Washington DC were all battling to get the fight. My thoughts were that they were not even boxing people, and with all the fights and experience I had in the business, why couldn't I do it?

"My first step was to reach out to my friend Tommy Patrick, the administrator for the State of Tennessee Boxing and Racing Division. Tommy and I had been close friend for years, and I knew he would have my back and help me get it done. We met for weeks at a truck stop off of I-Forty to come up with an effective game plan—and we did.

"We found out early Mike would be granted a license to fight in the state. We were now players in the game. I reached out to Shelly Finkel and told him the news, and during that same conversation we talked about being able to secure the funding for the site fee. That's when it really hit me I was at the make-or-break point—Can I find someone to believe in us enough to loan the twelve-point-five million dollars?

"After a few attempts that did not pan out, which included a former friend telling me that he had people that were interested in putting up money for me, at that point in time, we were all supposed to meet at the Outback Steakhouse on a Sunday night in which I would call Shelly and inform him that I was one step closer to getting it done. However, I could not have been any more wrong or depressed. Unfortunately, none of the so-called investors showed up.

"My mind was racing, and for the first time in this process, I had begun to doubt myself. My mind went into overdrive, thinking of anyone I had met in my life that would roll the dice for us. While at the Outback, I remembered a guy at the fitness center I had met who had told me just a few weeks before he was interested in investing in Prize Fight [Young's promotion company], as he had heard we put on some real good local fights. I jumped up from the table and immediately called over at the fitness center and explained to Ed Appleby that I needed Mike Lampley's cell phone number right away.

"Ed knew what I was up to and had been very supportive of my efforts. He called me a few minutes later with Mike's number. I was just completely honest with Mike and let him know this had to be done immediately if we were to land the fight. Mike was a big fight fan already, so half the battle was already won.

"I met with Mike the next day, along with my brother Russ, for dinner. By this time, news had begun to leak out that Nashville was in the mix to land the fight and that Mike had already been granted his license. The news ended up making the headlines in *The Tennessean* newspaper and was all over the TV. People and politicians were already taking sides — the fight was the talk of the town.

"Meanwhile, Mike went to work on securing the funding. Russ and I walked away from the meeting with different feelings. Russ had an MBA and was working in a bank as a loan officer, was a former pro football player as a quarterback and was probably the sharpest guy I knew. I trusted in no one more than him, and that's why he has always been the brain behind our company. Russ told me that he had a feeling Mike was going to come through.

"I, on the other hand, had my doubts, which is why to this day I'll never understand why I was telling the media we were ready to bring 'the biggest sporting event ever to the city.' The question was: Where in Nashville is the fight going to be?

"Well, there were only two logical places, the Gaylord Entertainment Center or the Titans' stadium.

"First, I met with the Titans executives about putting the fight in their stadium, and the media ran with it. Actually, the Titans were receptive to the idea—all except Bud Adams, the owner. He played it out in the media over the next few days as it dominated everyone's attention. Then came his decision day, when Adams would make his announcement on a local radio show. As I was driving to the fitness center for work that afternoon, he got on the radio and announced that he had decided 'No way, Jose,' as it was a moral issue with him.

"I truly believe he used it as a public relations tool to endear him to the city, which he didn't even live in. In the end, he could do whatever he wanted anyway. The city had given him the management rights to the stadium, which was publicly funded and he privately managed. The city was really torn, asking, How could Bud Adams have so much control over what went into the stadium when we were all paying for it anyway?

"Bud had his supporters, too, which went all the way to the top. The mayor said if we reached second base in the negotiations he would move to put a stop to it. This was certainly the lowest point of my career, having been humiliated on radio. Maybe it was for the best, though, as it was the perfect out for me since I didn't have the funding in place yet anyway.

"I went into work that day so depressed I couldn't have helped anybody through a workout if my life had depended on it. About two hours into my shift, I received a phone call from Mike informing me that he had secured the funding — twelve-point-five million — and that he himself would cover the expenses. I went from zero to a hundred in seconds.

"I immediately called some contacts in Memphis to see if they would be receptive about hosting the fight. The Pyramid was open for June eighth, and word got back to me within an hour that Mayor Herenton wanted the fight. We had done it!

"Ed let me off work that night so I could go over to Memphis. They welcomed us with open arms and were excited about having the fight come there, as they knew the benefits for the city. I ended up buying a house here in April of two-thousand-two and have been here ever since. Also, Russ ended up leaving the bank and relocating here as well.

"Since Lewis-Tyson, there have been five world title fights here, and the two-thousand-four Olympic Trials, with more on the way. Our monthly casino shows sell out every time, we've opened a gym, and enjoy a nice office that serves as our headquarters. The city and the state have been the recipient of an influx of sixty-five million dollars in tourism, city and state taxes. The boxing commission has gone from running in the red every year to being able to operate in the black for years to come.

"People have asked me over the years if I am bitter at the way Nashville treated one of their own. I would not be completely honest if I said it didn't bother me, because it did. However, I always go back to what a friend once told me, that the best revenge is success. In this case, I thank God on a continual basis that he had blessed Prize Fight and allowed it to happen."

Thanks in large part to Brian Young, June 8 was the date. It would be staged in The Pyramid, which was actually the world's third tallest pyramid, though this one was constructed out of glass and steel. The one man who deserved the most credit for saving the event was Young.

"There have been some rumors that some other people had something to do with it," said Tyson advisor Shelly Finkel. "But the reason we are coming to Memphis is because Brian Young pursued it."

Mayor Willie W. Herenton said in the Memphis *Commercial-Appeal*, "I'm praying that we have a great fight. And that we can pull this off without embarrassment to anyone. It has a lot of upside, but if we don't execute well, it has a downside, too."

The fight promised to be a boon for Memphis. Tickets were selling. Quickly, gross ticket sales were $23.9 million. That translated into sales tax revenue alone of $1.8 million. Not bad for a local economy that had been struggling. Unemployment had risen to 5.6% in January 2002, the highest level since June 1995, and about 22% more Memphians filed for bankruptcy protection in the twelve months that ended March 31 compared to the prior year.

Mayor Herenton figured approximately 40,000 people would visit Memphis for Lewis-Tyson. The Memphis Convention and Visitor's Bureau estimated visitors would spend as much as $50 million on blues music, barbecues and trips to Graceland.

"This fight is bigger than Mike Tyson," Herenton told the Memphis *Commercial-Appeal*. "It's about a sporting attraction that's going to yield great economic returns."

A ton of work was still to be done. A lot of promises would need to be fulfilled. Memphis was an unproven host. Tyson was still very much an unpredictable entity. Could anything else possibly go wrong?

VII

Tyson Turbulence in Maui

Let them hate me, just so long as they
fear me.

— Accius

Logistics for the fight were falling into place. Contracts called for $17.5 million each for Tyson and Lewis, plus a portion of the pay-per-view revenues. The potential snag of HBO and Showtime failing to reach accord was eliminated — both networks agreed to share PPV revenues, which were expected to reach $100 million. If Lewis won, HBO would win rebroadcast rights. If Tyson won, Showtime did.

Tyson released a statement on his acceptance of the challenge.

"Lennox made me an offer I cannot refuse, and it's time to give the people what they want. The heavyweight championship is my destiny. And I want those belts around my waist again. So, keep taking those acting lessons, Lennox, 'cause your next role will be playing

Cinderella. And I'm going to break your little glass chin."

There were suspicions, though, that one of the reasons for Tyson's controversial behavior was that, deep down, he was a reluctant participant in this fight. That he was just barely complying only because he was reportedly in dire need of the payday to satisfy an army of creditors. Trainer Tommy Brooks was let go on the eve of the infamous press conference in January, most likely because of a money dispute.

Brooks said, "I think Mike wants to fight Lewis. But when you've amassed the amount of money that Mike has, and they're telling you you're only going to earn kibbles and bits from here on out, why should you make the effort?"

What Brooks meant was, Why should Tyson fight his heart out if he was only going to see a small percentage of the $17.5 million, after creditors collected their cuts?

Tyson's finances were reported to be in serious disarray. A year after buying a 56,000-square-foot man-sion in Farmington, Connecticut, for $2.8 million, he tried to sell it for $22 million. The home, which has twenty bedrooms, thirty-eight bathrooms, an Olympic-size pool, a shooting range and a nightclub, didn't attract any buyers. So, Tyson dropped the asking price to $13 million and later to $5 million before taking it off the market in the summer of 2001. One published report claimed he only stayed in the house once.

Like his enormous estate in Connecticut, Tyson's value had depreciated. Although his ring earnings have been estimated at greater than $200 million, some of his former friends and managers were now claiming he was extremely deep into debt. His bankroll had been diminished by careless spending, bad management and marital problems.

Tyson owed $12 million to Viacom Inc.'s Showtime Networks, which has a multi-fight agreement with the boxer, *Sports Illustrated* reported, citing "industry insiders." He also owed $2.5 million to his former promoter, America Presents, and the estate of Bill Daniels, the late cable television pioneer who helped finance the company, according to the Las Vegas *Review-Journal* newspaper.

In 1998, the Internal Revenue Service placed liens on Tyson's homes in Ohio, Connecticut and Las Vegas because he owed the federal government $6.4 million in taxes. The liens were removed the following year, and Tyson later sold his Ohio home for $1.3 million; but he still owed about $74,000 in property taxes and local fees on his Connecticut home, according to the Farmington tax collector.

Bill Cayton, Tyson's former manager, speculated that Mike could face hard times.

"I think he needs a few more big paydays to get back in the black," said Cayton, who had a bitter split with Tyson in 1988. Shelly Finkel, Tyson's current adviser, denied that the boxer is broke, but he repeatedly declined to discuss details about Tyson's finances.

Tyson has acknowledged that his spending sprees on expensive cars, jewelry, homes, pet lions and tigers and other luxury items over the years have drained his bank account. Documents compiled for Tyson's $100 million lawsuit against his former promoter Don King reflect Iron Mike's extravagant lifestyle. From 1995 to 1997, he spent $4.5 million on cars and motorcycles; $748,000 on lawn care for his three homes; $412,000 on his pet pigeons, lions and tigers; $411,000 on one birthday party and $240,000 on pagers and mobile phones.

Many of Tyson's former friends and business associates blame Don King for the fighter's financial woes. In his 1998 lawsuit against King (for $100 million, which was eventually settled in 2004 for between $10-15 million), Tyson claimed his money was used to pay the promoter's personal expenses and to give King's relatives high-paying jobs. The suit also claims that King and former co-managers John Horne and Rory Holloway ended up getting about fifty percent of Tyson's earnings — far, far more than traditional arrangements where managers get about a thirty-three percent cut. In addition, the suit says King used his connection with Tyson to get $42 million from Showtime for other fighters without sharing any of the money with Tyson. Adding to the intrigue is the fact that King has openly bragged to the media how he has twice paid tax bills that exceeded $30 million.

Tyson's finances were in decline and so, too, were his training habits. Former trainer Brooks was sounding considerably less loyal to Team Tyson as the weeks went by.

"I'm relieved that I don't have to deal with the idiots around him anymore," said Brooks in *Boxing Update*. "You've got backstabbers undermining what you're trying to accomplish in the gym. A majority of them can't see the big picture. Tyson has been cutting corners for so long, I'm not sure he knows another way now. I'm regretful a guy with so much talent and ability went down the tubes."

Tyson named Ronnie Shields as his new lead trainer on April 11. Shields would join Stacey McKinley and Jay Bright.

Tyson arrived in Maui for his training camp in late April. He and his group stayed in a beachfront villa at Fairmont Kea Lani in Wailea for $1,500 a night. There were no strip clubs in Maui to distract the ex-champ.

"I found that out once I got here," Tyson said in *Boxing Update*. "I'm here to do a job. I work as hard as I play. It was a good idea coming here. I came here one time when I was married [to Monica], and I didn't have a good time. My main objective now is to be professional. But kill him. That's what it comes to. He should want to kill me because I want to kill him. But I still love him."

Two months before the fight, Tyson was in good condition and in good spirits, at least for the time being. That changed when some members of the media were invited to interview him. Dan Klores Communications was organizing a week of media interviews to show Tyson was "changed" and ready for the fight. This was designed to help boost ticket and pay-per-view sales.

Of course, there would be restrictions on the topics to be discussed. No reporter could ask anything about the press conference debacle. Only questions about the fight were allowed.

"I'm not in the mood to be upset and go into a tirade," Mike said. "Maybe in a few weeks I will be. I can't foresee losing. I can't even conceive the fact of losing, not in my sleep, nothing."

Tyson was asked how he would get ready for the fight.

"How would *you* get ready for a fight?" he shot back. "I've been uncomfortable all my life. This should be fun. The fight will be fun. So, why shouldn't this be fun? I've just got to get in proper preparation psychologically. Be hungry and determined. But it's just a fight."

Things seemed to be running smoothly in the Tyson

camp—so far, so good. But the mood would soon change. My, oh, my, would it change.

Tyson did an interview on national US television, later published in numerous boxing magazines, and articulated some astonishingly candid revelations. Here's a sampling:

> No, the title doesn't deserve to be treated with respect because the title is like a woman…"Fuck you, I'm so beautiful I can get the next man with more money, with a better body"…I'm just—part of it's money, part of it's greed…Am I an animal? If necessary, it depends on what situation [I'm] in…No, Desiree Washington raped *me*, okay?…But how can somebody truly love a guy like me that has all this money?…How do you get to his essence, when his essence is only money?…Let me live my life because I'm not going to let these people just tear me apart and the guys try to label me…I don't think I'm evil, but I think I'm capable of being evil like everyone else…I'm surprised I'm not suicidal…I haven't killed myself, but I wouldn't do that. I prefer to kill someone else than to kill myself.

How could you hate Mike Tyson after reading those admissions? Someone once said, "Show me a hero and I'll show you a tragedy." Mike Tyson seems sometimes like a tragic hero.

Boxing against Lennox Lewis appeared to be only one of a myriad of personal problems for Tyson. And fighting Lennox Lewis with a clear, healthy mind would be hard enough as it is. But boxing is still what Mike Tyson probably does best in this world.

The episode in Hawaii was not finished yet, though. There was still more antisocial behavior to come from the supposedly "changed" Tyson.

At a gym interview session, Tyson was sitting with a group of reporters, one an attractive female.

"I normally don't do interviews with women unless I fornicate with them," Tyson said. "So you shouldn't talk anymore."

Tyson directed that remark to a young reporter named Josie Karp from CNN. She managed to keep her composure and asked another question. Mike Tyson turned his back on her. Not one of the fifteen or so other men in the room raised a single word of protest. No one would stand up to Tyson. Heck, if you did, your physical well-being could be altered permanently.

Tyson was not finished. "I wish that you guys had children so I could kick them in the fucking head or stomp on their testicles so you could feel my pain because that's the pain I have waking up every day."

After it was over, Tyson's handlers tried to smooth things over with Karp by offering her a one-on-one. She was reluctant at first but decided to accept.

"Where you from?" Tyson asked her.

"Boston," Karp replied.

"That means you hate niggers," Tyson somehow concluded. That launched him into another diatribe, against the media and white people. Tyson was well aware Karp was a member of both those groups. "But I still want you to suck my dick," he told her.

Tyson's handlers stood close by, smiling as usual. Only Muhammad Siddeeq, Tyson's spiritual advisor since the Indiana incarceration, had the decency to apologize to Karp after the episode ended.

A few days later, Ronnie Shields did an interview with columnist Wallace Matthews, then of *The New York Post* (now with *New York Newsday*).

"I didn't know this man from Adam when I first got here," Shields said about his employer, Tyson. "But from what I've seen, it's ridiculous how people say this and that about him. I can't believe this is the same person I've heard about. He's so nice, so gentle. He just wants people to respect him. Really, he's been a pleasure."

Shields was in that same room when Tyson disrespected the female TV reporter. He never even mentioned it in the interview.

Dan Klores, the high-powered New York publicist who had represented Tyson since the "Bite Fight" of 1997, had finally seen and heard enough. He was finished with Tyson.

"I'm going to tell [Showtime Network president] Matt Blank we're resigning immediately," Klores said to Matthews. "Why do I need this?"

VIII

Supreme and Serene in the Poconos

There is no joy but calm.

— Tennyson

Lennox arrived at his favorite training grounds — the Caesars Brookdale Resort — on Friday, April 12. It was a special place for Lewis. He's never lost a fight after training there.

"I like the sereneness, the freshness, the mountains. No traffic. You can wake up and jog the trails and see deer. I like that."

Located in the mountains of eastern Pennsylvania, the setting is a perfect one for a boxing training camp. Not far away, about an hour southwest, was Muhammad Ali's permanent training camp at Deer Lake.

The champion actually enjoyed the rigors of training camp.

"He loves training camp," said Steward. "He loves the training routine. He's still an athlete. Some boxers, by the age of the late thirties, are struggling. They're getting hit easily in training. They're getting knocked around. But Lennox is still at the top of his game. Very rarely does he get hit. In training camp, he doesn't get hit. To him it's like chess. He makes his job look easy."

As a master champion, Lewis knew how to prepare and peak for a fight. Since 1992, whenever I've seen him, whether he's had a fight scheduled or not, Lewis has always appeared to be in fighting shape, or very close to it. This is an important, tell-tale sign of the great fighters, who embrace the task of training earnestly, as opposed to treating it as drudgery.

The purpose in the Poconos was to transform and recreate his body and soul through exercise, punishment and repetition. Each day, he would work on the punching bags, certain technical aspects, stretching and flexibility, swimming, lifting weights, jumping rope. The softness of comfort and contentedness would be metamorphosed into a lean, mean, starved fighting machine. By June it would all be honed down and peaked. Lewis would be at his physical zenith, at his animalistic, primal best.

The champion and his team rented a cluster of cabins in the woods, just a short walk from the lake. As usual, the champ's mom would handle cooking chores. Some of her son's favorites were Caribbean dishes: plantains, curried chicken, rice, peas, spaghetti and apple pie.

Scott DeMercado of Jamaica is part of the training team and security. He is the guy who does the stretching routine with Lennox before every workout. The champ's flexibility, especially in the shoulder area, is an impressive sight. Tennis great Pete Sampras has great shoulder agility as well. During his playing days, the seven-time

Wimbledon champion could touch his elbows to-gether—behind his back. Roger Federer is said to do yoga every day for an hour to enhance his flexibility.

Courtney Shand, a graduate in physical-training studies at Fanshawe College in Ontario, is in charge of Lennox's strength and fitness. Courtney and Lennox were classmates at Cameron Heights High School and teammates on the football team. Lennox was fullback, Courtney the tailback.

Harold "The Shadow" Knight is the senior member of Team Lewis and acts as the assistant to Steward. Knight has worked with Lennox since his pro debut. The Shadow was an outstanding boxer himself, having once lost a narrow decision on national television for the IBF Junior Lightweight title to Rocky Lockridge in 1988. Knight had to retire after that defeat—at the youthful age of 25—because of a cyst-like lesion that was detected on his brain. He is perfectly healthy today, he just can't box anymore.

Now Knight locates and hires the most suitable spar-ring partners, helps with strategies, among other duties. He also has brought in his fine young undefeated heavyweight Malik Scott. Lennox has taken Scott under his wing, and you can often see the champ giving him instruction.

Rounding out the camp were longtime friends like Patrick Drayton of London, who helps with security, is a running mate, and prepares the underground English techno garage music for the workouts, among other du-ties. Ron Hepburn from Canada helps with security and is a running mate. Joe Dunbar is a sports physiologist and is the resident expert on nutrition, vitamins, sup-plements and running. Kojo Amoafo organizes all of

Lennox's media interviews, quite a consuming task considering the countless international requests for the heavyweight champion's thoughts and opinions on various matters.

Well-rounded athleticism is not the norm for the top boxers. Like a true artist, the champion boxer must "forsake all cares and sadness, save for thy art." There are some notable exceptions, though—Sugar Ray Leonard was one. He was very adept at many sports, such as golf, tennis, basketball, football and baseball. Roy Jones, of course, has played professional minor league basketball. Rocky Marciano was a hard-hitting football linebacker, and even had a baseball tryout with the Chicago Cubs.

But many of the great boxers were mediocre or even poor at other sporting activities. Muhammad Ali, for instance, could do no other sport well except boxing. In fact, I've heard it said that Ali had no basketball talent to speak of. Another example was Joe Frazier, who participated in the inaugural 1973 Superstars competition on ABC's *Wide World of Sports*. Howard Cosell and Jim McKay watched as Frazier almost drowned during the swimming heats. He had to be helped from the pool.

Lennox Lewis was a natural, gifted athlete. He excelled at many sports: soccer, golf, tennis, football, basketball, pool, bowling, baseball, softball, paintball, knife-throwing and chess. Courtney Shand told me Lennox still holds the high school javelin record in Ontario.

Overall, it is well-known in boxing that Team Lewis is a close-knit, low-key group of good people. You have never heard of them mouthing off or finding trouble with the law like some of the other boxing entourages. The Lewis support team all emote quiet dignity, class and professionalism, a reflection of the champion himself.

The atmosphere of Lennox's camp has the feel of what the ideal boxing training camp should be—all business and hard work. No controversy. No disturbances. And definitely no snapshot pictures in the newspapers of smoking pot out of a pipe under the Hawaiian palm trees like Tyson was allegedly photographed doing.

Lewis's regimen is simple. He runs in the still of the dark morning at five. He trains in the afternoon, usually around two or three. Almost all of the workouts are closed to the local vacationers by a heavy curtain. Lewis's free time is occupied by listening to music, chess—sometimes two games at once—billiards, table tennis, court tennis and bike rides. Wednesdays and Sundays are days off for everyone.

The gym is about a one-minute van ride over to the other side of the lake, to the main building complex that houses registration, the restaurant, bar, heated swimming pools, tennis courts, volleyball courts and video game rooms. The boxing gym is set up in the rollerskating rink, which is adjacent to the indoor mini golf course and the indoor pool. The gym room has one ring, a weight bench and dumbells, jumprope mirror, sit-up benches, pull-up bar, speed and heavy bags.

Some of Lewis's personal training quirks are that he always puts his right glove on first. The room must always be heated at eighty-five degrees. And he only takes thirty seconds—not a full minute—to rest between sparring rounds.

I talked with two people who actually shared a ring with Lewis. Former IBF Cruiserweight Champion Glenn

McCrory from Newcastle, England, now a well-respected TV commentator in Great Britain, fought Lewis in Kensington in 1991. He spoke of that match still almost in awe, more than a decade later.

"The thing about Lewis is, he's so strong physically," McCrory told me. "In our fight, Lennox came right out and attacked me, because of some comments I had made to the media. I couldn't believe how fuckin' strong the guy was. And I've sparred with Tyson, McCall, Golota, everybody. Lennox threw me around like I was a rag doll. I had no chance."

McCrory didn't last two rounds. And today Lewis weighed around two-fifty—a solid two-fifty—compared to two-thirty-one for that fight with McCrory.

Incidentally, the two are now friends who keep in contact. McCrory shared a story about how he ran into his old nemesis at a nightclub in Miami a few years ago.

"Lennox invited us to play soccer on the beach the next morning. Sure enough, at ten a.m., Lennox and his friends came to the hotel and basically dragged me out of bed. And we went out and played soccer on the beach. It had to be around a hundred degrees that day."

Scott LeDoux, a former heavyweight contender, also climbed into the ring with Lewis. Now in his fifties, LeDoux, who unsuccessfully challenged Larry Holmes for the WBC title in 1980, filmed a feature segment for ESPN2's *Friday Night Fights* about sparring with Lewis. Like McCrory, you could hear a tone of wonder in his voice when discussing Lewis.

"Well, I was surprised, shocked about how difficult he was to trap, get in the corner," said LeDoux. "He's good at leaning back on his heels. He gets you to reach, then he fires a right hand down the chute. It hurt me. My ribs were hurt for six weeks. He whacked me good. I told him not to pull any punches. I said to him, If you knock me out, you'll be the first! I've never been knocked out. It'd be a new experience."

"Anywhere the guy hits you — the arms, shoulders — he hurts you. His jabs hurt you. I mean, you feel it. He is just so strong. And he is very good at keeping out of punching range. He has great sense about measuring distance. He is excellent defensively. People don't realize how good he is defensively. He has tremendous footwork. You go to punch him and he just leans back, way back, out of range. Defensively, he's very under-rated."

Lewis develops and perfects his sharpness by participating in all types of competitions during training camp. Competition in any form is a central theme to the Lewis camp. Lewis once had a three-point shot contest against Oscar De La Hoya when they trained together under Steward at Big Bear in the late 90's. (If my secret source is correct, it was the Golden Boy who came out the victor.)

After a hard day's work in the gym, there's still plenty more athletic activities for Lewis after dinner.

"Evenings in our camp are punctuated with the long-standing fortnightly chess, ping-pong and pool leagues," informed Kojo Amoafo. "These chess games are sometimes heated with arguments over moves that are retracted. Overall, this camp has been as relaxed as any we've had. Lennox looked almost the finished product before the end of April. He is such a perfectionist that Emanuel Steward and Harold Knight have to keep him on a leash."

The conversation turned to discussing the man they were all there preparing to vanquish.

"We all thought it was quite interesting, the viewings and publications of Mike Tyson's interviews with reporters and his unleashing of some very controversial and unwelcoming comments towards visiting press at his camp," wrote Amoafo in a post at www.lennoxlewis.com. "Lennox, in all his interviews, has reiterated that he's also had an unprivileged up-bringing, but sought to do something better for himself in life. He detracted from self-pity and chose to look for positive role models and self-betterment. Respect and integrity are some of the qualities he aspired to in all aspects of life, especially towards women."

After Tyson revealed his tortured soul at his camp, Lewis was ready to respond publicly on his first media day on May 7. He was wearing a white FUBU baseball-style jersey with "Memphis" scripted on the front.

"In a sense, I don't think he really wants to fight, with some of the things he says." Lewis speculated. "Seriously, I think a lot of the times, he's totally talking for his own benefit. He's trying to make himself out to be some kind of bad man—that he can say and do whatever he wants. But he's going to learn that there are repercussions."

"When Mike Tyson makes a comment, I don't take it one hundred percent. Because I realize he is a disturbed person, like a madman talking," Lewis continued. "I believe these antics of his are just to cloud the public's mind of his own fears. He says I do not fear him, and he's right. I don't. He's an imbecile when it comes to certain comments. I think Tyson is just so frustrated with his life now. If you listen, his thought patterns are all jumbled. I don't think he's off his head but he may be looking for an excuse not to fight me.

"He should watch what he says. His words certainly

don't upset me but they might upset his kids when they hear them on TV. I think he's mentally and physically fit, but his antics outside the ring sound like a cartoon character. When he was incarcerated, he said he was reading. It sounds like he was reading comic books."

Tyson's unusual mental state in Hawaii, feigned or not, was not intimidating Lewis in any way.

"I'm a fighter, he's a biter. I'm going to insist he has a big lunch and a big dinner before he steps in there," the champion joked to the media assemblage of about seventy-five as he sat on the ring apron. "And I'm going to have my hair pinned back so he can't pull it out. I don't know what else he can possibly do. If he's choosing to come in and bite and scratch and kick, I'm going to be a better man and not do those things back. I'm a man of honor."

Are you concerned at all, with some of the things he's saying?

"I've heard all of those words before," Lewis answered, smiling easily. "That's how he carries on. After a while, we need to self-teach. He sounds like a cartoon character when he says those things. To me, it's just coming from an ignorant person. That's the way he wants to make himself out to be. He says he likes to be in jail. Who likes to be in jail?"

Doesn't it worry you when Tyson says he would like to "kill" you?

Lewis laughed. "Mike Tyson says a lot of stuff, and none of it really has come true. I think he's talking for his own benefit. He said things about Evander Holyfield and what he wanted to do, but did he go in there and do it? No."

Lewis admitted he considered denying Tyson the title shot after Tyson bit him on the leg.

"At one point, I thought the best way to punish Tyson would be to not fight him. When he bit, I thought, okay, he's definitely trying to get out of the fight. But I wanted him to get out of the fight on its own merits, not with me helping the situation. So I never said anything."

Listening to the classy champion speak in his thoughtful, intelligent manner, the idea came to mind of Lewis possibly losing. This was frightening. How would it impact the world if "good" were to be defeated by "evil?" If naughty and nasty were to win out over pleasant and nice? So much more than money and titles was at stake here. This fight would be the latest, modern version of the ancient battle between Good and Evil.

"Lennox wants to knock out Mike Tyson in the worst way," Steward promised. "I've only met one other fighter I've been involved with who had that same desire. That was Holyfield[8]. We have that situation where emotions are involved, and emotions make great events — Hagler-Leonard, Hagler-Hearns. The emotions are going to explode in this fight."

Steward and Lewis are not only business associates but also close friends and get along extremely well. They have a loyal and rock-solid connection. Above all, they are pals who enjoy each other's company and have a friendship that extends outside of the sport, which is not typical in boxing. Even between fights, Steward likes to stay in close contact with his boxers. He went fishing with Julio Cesar Chavez in Mexico. He went dancing at night with Evander Holyfield. He's spent time in sporting and leisure activities with Lennox and his friends in

---

[8] Steward trained Holyfield for one fight, the Bowe rematch Holyfield won in 1993

Canada and England. Steward says he likes to get to know the fighter, see how and where he lives.

While Steward is considered by many as the most accomplished trainer in boxing and has been a leading figure in the sport since 1980, not many people know that he was a top amateur fighter. Emanuel Steward was born on July 7, 1944, in Welch, West Virginia. He moved to Detroit at age 11 when his parents divorced, and soon took up boxing. He won the Detroit Golden Gloves in 1962 and 1963. He became one of the best amateur boxers in the country by winning the National Golden Gloves Tournament of Champions at Chicago Stadium in 1963.

But he never felt comfortable about punching for pay, mainly because he says he never could quite find the right manager to guide him through the shark-infested world of pro-boxing. So, he never turned professional.

But his vast knowledge of boxing would not go to waste. Steward's career as a boxing trainer began a few years later, when he started to train his younger brother, James, in 1970. They went to the nearest boxing gym they could find in Detroit—the Kronk Recreation Center, located at 5555 McGraw Street on Detroit's southwest side. The building was named after a Detroit City councilman named John Kronk. Upstairs at the Kronk Rec Center, kids played games and retirees enjoyed bingo and square-dancing. Down the steel stairs in the basement, kids learned boxing. After only five months of coaching from his brother, James won the Detroit Golden Gloves tournament. In 1971, Emanuel accepted the part-time position as head coach of the Kronk Recreation Center's boxing program, for $35 a week.

Later that year, James Steward and six other novice

Kronk boxers—Louis Holland, Edward Gaston Jr., Demond Hickman, James Stokes, Wilson Bell, and Robert Johnson—entered the Detroit Golden Gloves. The Kronk team—coached by Emanuel Steward—scored twenty-one consecutive victories and captured the team title. Thus, the Kronk dynasty had begun.

Soon after, though, that first Kronk team disbanded as many of the young men joined the military. Steward then focused all his training energies on one particular young boxer named Bernard Mays. Mays became a legend in amateur boxing, winning National AAU and Junior Olympic titles, even being named Tournament Outstanding Boxer each time. At twelve, Mays was already boxing in main events before sold-out crowds at amateur shows.[9]

The success of the young prodigy Bernard "Super Bad" Mays began to draw many other junior boxers to Emanuel Steward and the spartan basement gym at the Kronk Recreation Center. Thomas Hearns and Duane Thomas, both future world champions, were among the curious visitors. The list of talented boxers that honed their skills under the tutelage of Steward at Kronk during this period is extraordinary—Milton McCrory, Caveman Lee, Mickey Goodwin, Dwain Bonds, Jimmy Paul, Frank Tate, Steve McCrory, to name a few. Steward was like an oracle with a magical ability to recognize and then develop the raw talent.

Steward and the bright red-and-yellow colors of the Kronk team first came into national prominence on March 2, 1980, when his fighter Hilmer Kenty captured

---

[9] Mays never fulfilled his enormous professional potential as he allegedly ruined his future because of alcohol and drug problems.

the WBA Lightweight title on national television by knockout from Ernesto Espana in a sold-out Joe Louis Arena in Detroit. The great man himself, Joe Louis, was even there at ringside. Kenty was Steward's first world champion.

Eight months later, also in Detroit, with Muhammad Ali sitting at ringside, Thomas "Hitman" Hearns stopped Jose "Pipino" Cuevas in the second round with a devastating right, and Steward had his second world champion—and first boxing superstar.

Sports Illustrated did a story on Hearns and Steward, calling Emanuel "the hottest trainer in boxing...and one respected for his independence and integrity." Many more boxers came to Kronk to practice at their craft, to draw inspiration from the world-renowned atmosphere, including Mark Breland, Pernell Whitaker and Tyrell Biggs, who all prepared at Kronk before they each won Olympic gold medals in 1984. Original Kronk members Frank Tate and Steve McCrory also won gold in Los Angeles. Over the years Steward has trained, at one time or another, Evander Holyfield, Prince Naseem Hamed, Oscar De La Hoya, Michael Moorer, Graciano Rocchigiani, Oliver McCall, Welcome N'cita, John David Jackson, Jeff Fenech, Miguel Angel Gonzalez, Leeonzer Barber, Jermain Taylor, Kermit Cintron, Wladimir Klitschko and Gaby Canizales.

Steward's success and popularity has also earned him a position as a member of the distinguished HBO broadcast team with Jim Lampley and Larry Merchant. He was hired by Wesley Snipes and Eminem to teach them boxing techniques for film roles.

Lennox Lewis could have no better man beside him than Steward as he prepared for this, the fight of his life.

Steward knew conquering Tyson was critically important to the career legacy of Lewis. There would be no slip-ups or corners cut.

"We're preparing for the Tyson we saw in eighty-eight, eighty-nine," Steward said. "Lennox knows he has to be more careful, but he can only be so careful. He can't try and outbox Tyson. All of his wins go down the drain with a loss to Tyson.

"Like Alexis Arguello had a great, great career, but what you most remember about his career is the two losses at the end to Aaron Pryor. It's sad but true. Lennox says he's not going to let twenty-five years go down the drain for some little guy like Mike Tyson. After his career is over, Lennox is going to be remembered for the Rahman rematch and the Tyson fight.

"If Tyson is coming back to his foundation, the way he used to be, he will be a strong, competitive guy. He is a big enough threat right now, with his tremendous punching power and the intensity he brings to a fight. Lennox has to be aggressive in a very special way. He has to take control and never let Mike get his full confidence back, because, deep down, I feel Mike will be at his very best for this fight.

"Lennox has been ready. He is as calm and relaxed as he's ever been for any of his fights. Tyson is the one who refused to fight Lewis. Lennox is not afraid of Tyson, which is something Tyson is not used to. This is probably the first time in a long time that Tyson will be fighting someone that is not afraid of him. To my knowledge, the only fighters that fought Tyson in the past who were not afraid of him and had the talent, all beat him. Holyfield definitely was not afraid. And Buster Douglas was not."

Steward's musings are fascinating to listen to. "I do not think Tyson has won a prizefight in the last five years, with secondary competition," he said. "Lennox is at his peak as a fighter. Tyson is in a situation where he has nothing to do but to fight Lewis because of monetary reasons and public pressure. I think Tyson is going to come out and give it his all, but Lewis is too much for him. I think Tyson is going to rise as far as he can go, but it's not going to be enough.

"It could even be a very short fight, maybe even a round or two. We've been watching films of short fights, like Hearns-Duran, Johansson-Patterson, Liston-Patterson. Like Lennox said, You can learn a lot from watching a short fight."

Though Lennox is very civilized and dignified at all times, his courteous manner belies a primal killer instinct in competition. "People don't realize it but Lennox's background in Canada was that he was a street thug," said Steward. "He's got this dark side to him that he doesn't let out too often. This fight has brought that out in him.

"I think it's great, in a way. One of my biggest problems with Lennox is he has been too passive, too much of a thinker, too analytical. This fight here, he's got this burning desire to knock Mike Tyson out. I've never seen that in him before."

Tyson's trainers responded quickly, as if hurt by the words that were coming out of Pennsylvania. They did not take the high ground.

"I'm very glad if Lennox is very relaxed for this fight," Ronnie Shields said. "That is a positive sign that Lewis may stand and fight Tyson. Nobody in the world can stand up and fight Tyson. He is going to feel the wrath of Tyson's punches. Steward may be right about the fight ending in the first round. That might be all it takes for Tyson to knock out Lewis. If Lewis doesn't knock out Tyson early, you may see Lewis retreating. I would not be surprised to see Lewis stick his head out of the ropes and just keep on going."

Tyson's other trainer, Stacey McKinley, an appropriate representative for Tyson, threw some more darts at Lewis.

"This fight is only big on paper. In terms of the ring, it's just another fight. You have a great fighter going against a good fighter. You have a fighter with a good chin going against a fighter with a bad chin. You have a fighter who is mentally strong going against a guy who is mentally weak. You have a fighter with the biggest heart in boxing going up against a guy with a weak heart."

Former Heavyweight Champion Ingemar Johansson once told me of an old saying they had in Sweden about those who talked a lot: "The empty pot makes the most noise."

There were no questions that Steward would duck. He willingly discussed anything you asked him — even the issue of Lewis's chin, which had failed him twice, against Rahman and McCall.

"If people are concerned with Lewis's chin, I have no problem with Lewis's chin," he explained. "People should concern themselves with Tyson's chin. If Tyson gets hit with the punches Lewis put on Rahman, Grant and Golota, I'm wondering if Tyson can take a punch from a big, two hundred-fifty-pound man that punches with full force.

"Everybody is focused on Lewis being hit, and he is

preparing on getting hit in this fight. Lennox may have to outfight Tyson like he did against Ray Mercer. It could be that way, since Tyson has good head movement. The winner may be the guy who is in better condition, willing to take the punches and gut it out. Lennox's two losses were because he didn't really respect McCall or Rahman as much as he should have. Tyson he respects. But he totally wants to beat him. We worry about him actually attacking Mike. I'm seriously worried about that, and that we might get disqualified."

Lewis was truly eager to terminate Tyson. "I'm tired of Tyson's talk, of the attention he gets for simply being someone who can't take any control of his life or his career," he said. "And I'll be glad to see him coming into the ring because that's where it gets hard, where whatever you say doesn't mean a thing, and you have to be honest and just fight. I'm going to turn it on. I'm going to put down that American belief that Tyson is some kind of god of the ring. I'm going to say to the Americans who have not shown me much respect over the years, 'Hey, I'm really the very best.'"

Harold Knight also added his insights, in an interview with Steve Farhood of *Boxing Monthly* magazine from England.

"When we started in 1990, this is what we wanted—to fight Tyson. Now, twelve years later, it's here. I think Mike has doubts about his ability to beat Lennox, and Lennox is incredibly confident that he can beat Mike. Mike's intimidation doesn't work anymore. Those tactics don't work on Lennox, anyway.

"Look what happened in the second fight with Rahman. In the dressing room, we were all on the edge of our seats. We knew it was all over if Lennox lost that fight. And Lennox was the only calm one in the room. That's when I knew Lennox would win.

"I feel Mike will be dangerous for the first five rounds. We gotta stay away from him for a few rounds. Then again, the enigma that Lennox is, he could come right out and...I say to him all the time, 'You got Uzis and mortars and everything. So, why are you using a thirty-eight?' If he uses them, the fight won't go three rounds. But as Emanuel says, we don't know which Lennox will come out."

"It will be a battle of good versus evil," Lennox said, in his gentle but firm voice. There was conviction and certainty in his tone. And there was no doubt about who would come out on top. "The way I look at it, the good guy has to win. And the good guy will win."

IX

Fight Week In Memphis

Everything that deceives is said to enchant.

— Plato

Maybe the most qualified expert on earth to contemplate on Lewis-Tyson was Evander Holyfield. "The Real Deal" had already shared a ring twice each with both Tyson and Lewis. Somewhat surprisingly, though, Holyfield was decidedly favoring Tyson, even though he twice bested Tyson and twice came up short against Lewis.

But sometimes even the greatest of boxers can be the worst of predictors. For instance, Ali picked Michael Spinks to defeat Tyson, and Rocky Marciano went on record saying Liston would knock out Cassius Clay in one round in their first battle in Miami.

"Mike Tyson will knock out Lewis. Styles make fights," Holyfield forecast in *Boxing Update*. "You can't box Mike scared. If Lennox is going to knock Tyson out, he has to be aggressive. He has shown he can deal with a style like mine. But can he deal with Tyson's power? If Lennox does what he usually does — which is be cautious — if he retreats, he's in trouble. He doesn't go out there and take charge. He doesn't own the ground he walks on. That's why too many people don't buy him.

"Lennox likes to go back. And we know Tyson fights fighters real well when they go back. Lennox will try and hold and all that. But when Lennox takes time to get ready to punch, I think Tyson would bust him."

Holyfield's curious analysis was not on Lewis's mind when he arrived in Memphis on Friday afternoon, May 31. The champion was greeted to a hero's welcome. They organized a parade for him that day down Beale Street. Lewis promised the crowd, "Tyson's going to get knocked out. For real."

Mayor Herenton was on hand and gave Lennox the key to the city. In the parade, Lewis rode in a black Humvee limousine, preceded by a high school band, majorettes and dance teams. It was estimated that 10,000 people came out. A children's singing group called Watoto de Afrika performed a special number called "Ooooo Mr. Lewis." It went like this:

> Gather 'round 'cause Mr. Lewis
> Just came to town.
> He is the king of the ring
> 'Cause he can knock everybody down.

Lewis was enjoying the festivities. It was the first time he had ever received such adulation in America.

"I love it, I love Memphis."

After the parade ended in a local park, Lewis said

that they wouldn't see much more of him until fight time.

"I'm going to be focused on what I'm going to do to Mike Tyson."

He retired to his limo and was driven away, though not before one young woman who was bouncing up and down shouted for the champ to roll down his window. Instead, Lewis opened the door, let her in and gave her a quick hug.

Tyson dropped into Memphis without the grand entrance. He quietly arrived the same day by private jet at a small landing strip on the outskirts of Memphis International Airport. He stopped only to shake hands with Mayor Herenton. Tyson avoided the reporters and photographers who were waiting for him. Instead, he rented five movies from a video store and headed to a mansion northeast of Memphis.

The two fighters would conduct their final training sessions less than an hour down Route 61 in Tunica, Mississippi. Fitzgerald's Casino paid $1 million for the right to bill itself as the "Official Site of Mike Tyson." Tyson had fifty-two rooms reserved for his entourage, though many went unused. Lewis would hold his workouts just down the Tunica strip at Sam's Town Casino, though he was staying in a home inside a gated community in Memphis. He also used a gym at a nearby health and racquet club for his private exercises.

Of course, Tyson, with his natural flair for drama, could only go a couple of days without causing some sort of commotion. On Sunday, June 2, he was on his way to a fitness center when he suddenly got out of his SUV to confront a gay rights activist who was demonstrating. Jim Maynard, vice-chairman of Equality Tennessee, recalled the incident to the Memphis *Commercial-Appeal*. "I was shouting 'Stop Homophobia' and holding up my sign," he said. "And then [Tyson] just came up and hugged me. And he said he wasn't homophobic. I was totally shocked. I didn't really know what to do. So I just posed with Tyson and smiled for the cameras. It's a step in the right direction."

Tyson signed about twenty autographs before going inside for his workout. After the workout, he got in his vehicle, rolled down his window and said, "Listen, listen. I'm not homophobic. I told them I'm not homophobic. So, if I use a homophobic term, I'm not homophobic."

This was a new role for Tyson, that of the pacifist. Here was Iron Mike, The Baddest Man on the Planet, trying to appease a dispute instead of fighting it. Tyson had not shown that kind of civility in a very long time. This was a very good signal that the entire event would not deteriorate into another hideous carnage.

However, Team Lewis was still taking every possible precaution to ensure the fight came off properly. Because of Tyson's unpredictable and raucous ways at the January press conference, the champion used his leverage and insisted on a few changes to the original fight contract.

- After Lewis proved by DNA evidence that Tyson had, indeed, bitten him on the leg at the press conference, the bite wound up costing Tyson $335,000 of his fight purse. Should Tyson commit an "extraordinary foul" in the bout, Lewis will be entitled to $2.5 million more than the original purse of

$17.5 million. That money would be subtracted from Tyson's purse.

- If Lewis lost and Tyson won, Tyson was contractually obligated to fight Lewis in his first title defense. Should Lewis win, he was allowed one mandatory defense before meeting Tyson a second time.

- There would be no contact of any kind between the two fighters prior to the bout. For the first time in anyone's memory, the prefight news conference, weigh-in and prefight instructions will be carried out separately. Also, the traditional tapping of the gloves in ring center had been outlawed.

Lewis was satisfied with all the contract amendments negotiated by his legal team, led by Patrick English and Judd Burstein. He was making sure the fight would come off with some semblance of decorum. Meanwhile, the Tyson camp viewed Lewis as little more than a whiner.

"It's ridiculous some of the things Lewis has asked for," complained Shelly Finkel. "We agreed to it because we wanted the fight. All of this other stuff is a joke. But there is a day of reckoning coming. Mike thinks Lennox is a big baby. Me? I think some of this stuff is paranoia."

Assistant Tyson trainer Stacey McKinley sounded the most disenchanted by Lewis' contractual changes.

"When you're a coward, you put a lot of things in contracts. He said he doesn't want Mike looking at him. He said he don't want to be in the same restaurant, in the same Blockbuster. even. I say he's a real bitch. Tell him I say so. If Lewis was here today I'd spit in his face.

I'd spit in his eye. I want Mike to break ribs and break jaws. I want them to take Lennox Lewis out on a stretcher.

"Nobody tells Mike Tyson what to do. Don't people know that by now? I've been with him for nine years, and this is the best shape he's ever been in. I can see it in his eyes. He's vicious. He's a born fighter."

With colorful quotes like that to the swarm of reporters, McKinley was fast becoming one of the more renowned characters in the Tyson brigade. He looks the part, too, with his Mean Street eyes, shaven skull, full beard and no-nonsense demeanor. But he's actually a gentleman when not embroiled in the heat of the battle.

"Stacey has been the real force behind Mike for quite a while, even though they have brought several head trainers in there from time to time," said Steward. "He's the guy Mike looks up to. These other guys come and go because they don't have a lot of the same kind of significance to Mike that Stacey does."

If McKinley's sportsmanship capacities sometimes go over the line, at least his devoted loyalty to Tyson is commendable.

"Mike Tyson has done so much for me and my family, it is unbelievable," McKinley said to the Memphis *Commercial-Appeal*. "The houses and the condominiums, the new cars and all that stuff that I own, that has come from Mike Tyson. I appreciate the things Mike Tyson has done for me. I will be there for him all the way to the end."

"I respect Tyson's views on life and everything he does," McKinley said. "I support what he does. I respect that he tells people what he feels. His personal views in life are his own. In camp, he treats all of us with nothing but respect."

McKinley said he was introduced to Rory Holloway, Tyson's former co-manager. Tyson was in need of corner men for his return to the ring, and Holloway liked McKinley's work ethic.

"He told me, 'I'm going to put you in with Mike Tyson,'" McKinley said. "Even Don King didn't know. Mike told [Holloway] he didn't want any Angelo Dundee, he didn't want any Emanuel Steward. He just wanted a guy that was a hard worker."

McKinley guesses he has taken about 25,000 punches while training Tyson for thirteen fights over the last nine years. Fortunately, McKinley wears his trademark outfit of body padding to somewhat protect himself from the shots. And only once has he ever been hurt by Tyson while on the job. This happened just recently, while training for Lewis.

"It wasn't nowhere near his best shot," McKinley survived to tell. "He was working on a combination off the left hook. When he threw the left hook, it caught me on the right side of my lip and my mouth. My lip was swelling up like I don't know what. I was dizzy. Mike was real worried.'"

McKinley was there, as usual, on center stage at Tyson's scheduled workout for the media on Tuesday, June 4. Tyson appeared very fit as he came out shirtless. People stood on chairs in the crowded, non-air-conditioned room to get a glimpse of him. They didn't get to see much. All he did was hit the speed bag with McKinley barking out loud approval. He also practiced head movement reflexes on the slip bag. That was it. No statements, no sound bites for reporters. Tyson was all business now. Or more likely, no one wanted to take the risk of having Iron Mike chat with the media. A hell of a lot could go wrong if Mike got tagged with a question he didn't like. McKinley and Crocodile would do most of the talking from now on.

Derrick Jefferson was about the only Team Tyson guy who didn't seem to have any malice for Lewis. He is a fringe contender from Detroit who didn't know Mike Tyson before sparring with him in Hawaii.

"All I knew of Tyson before is what the fans knew, of what I saw on TV and what I read in papers and magazines," said the kindhearted and polite Jefferson. "He's a lot different guy than the impression I had. He's a good guy, a real good guy, and he's just fun to be around."

Mr. Crocodile was there, too. To do what he does best, which is to provide moral support and show off his preposterous vocal chords. Croc's contribution to the occasion consisted of his roaming the workout room and shouting his signature mantra: "Guerilla warfare!" He even created a special new catchphrase for the day: "Three more days and wake up!" Not sure what it meant, but when Crocodile shouts something a few times, you don't easily forget it. Crocodile, too, is a pretty friendly character when you talk with him one-on-one, much nicer than you would expect.

McKinley was amped up as the fight drew closer and taunted Lewis some more.

"Tell Lennox Lewis all hell is coming! All hell is coming! We're not worried about Lennox Lewis! If he second-guesses himself against Mike Tyson, he'll get knocked out! He's a coward. Remember that. It takes guts to get in the ring, but it takes heart to stay there. And he's got no heart."

Unlike his trainers, Tyson was quiet before exiting. His body language did not convey the look of a man who was destined to triumph on Saturday night. When all was said and done, he had given a somewhat lackluster performance in this twenty-minute training session. Some members of the gathered press described him as looking "listless." One headline even stated, "Listless Tyson Looks To Have Lost His Bite."

Lewis's press conference at Sam's Town on Wednesday was a study in contrast. It featured piped-in jazz music, cool central air and a buffet luncheon for the media. There was a short program of speakers before Lewis went through a forty-five-minute workout with the air conditioning turned off as the jazz was changed to reggae over the loudspeakers.

World Boxing Council President Jose Sulaiman raved about having Memphis as a site. He said when Memphis was first mentioned as a site for the fight, all he knew about Memphis and Tennessee was the Tennessee Waltz, Huckleberry Finn and Elvis Presley.

"When I flew into the city and saw the cleanliness and the architecture, saw it was a peaceful place and saw all the green," Sulaiman said, "I realized it was a great day."

Adrian Ogun, Lewis's business manager, was the emcee of the proceedings. He introduced all the players involved, which took quite a long time. And he reminded all that Saturday's fight had been such a long time in the making. That's right, it took nearly two decades. I wondered if any other fight in history had such an extended prelude—from sparring as teenagers to fighting for the richest prize in sport almost twenty years later. I couldn't think of any.

Emanuel Steward stepped up next. He was in fine form, as always.

"When I first got involved with Lennox Lewis back in 1994, I made the prediction that he had the ability and the potential to be the greatest heavyweight since Muhammad Ali. We are three days from that legacy being fulfilled."

"Lennox has always wanted to fight the best. I have very seldom seen a fighter who hasn't dodged anyone. Lennox Lewis has fought more undefeated challengers [than anyone] in the history of the division. Lennox is fighting better than ever. Tyson has been fighting second-rate fighters. This is the best today, and one of the greatest heavyweights of all time. And his record will be appreciated when he's gone.

"I know this man is phenomenal to train, and one of the finest human beings I ever dealt with. And that's why I chose to stay with him rather than go with Mike Tyson when I would have made three million dollars a fight. Lennox is worth being with because of the character in addition to the talent that he has. I think you are going to see a great fight.

"I think they have got Tyson back into a boxing mode now for the first time in years. And I think you're going to see the most fierce and determined and that best-that-he-can-be Mike Tyson come out in this fight. The fight not only has the ability of being a slugfest early but possibly going to the late rounds because I could see problems with the styles of each guy—because Mike Tyson has traditionally had problems with tall fighters. I don't know how he could have got any better.

"And Lennox may have problems, possibly, with the bob-and-weave style. It could end up being a great fight that ends up going down the stretch. The judges may end up being a big factor.

"But I think it's going to be an explosive fight. It has all of the elements that make a good fight and that, primarily, means emotions and determination. Not so much skills. I'm really looking forward to it. I've been involved in a lot of great fights. This is one that's really got me nervous. I'm waking up in the morning shadow-boxing myself. Anxious, I'm just getting excited about it.

"I love this. I love big-time fights. Lennox is the same way. That's why it's easy to beat him sometimes in what are perceived to be easy fights. But this is where Lennox goes to his best."

The audience was enthralled listening to the master boxing guru articulate his wisdom. Steward spoke about the blood sport with a stately benevolence. He is much more than a boxing trainer.

"When Lennox feels threatened — as he felt in the fight with Razor Ruddock, when they said he was overmatched — we saw what happened there. And also, he fought a guy named Golota, which everybody said, including my brother James, Oh, he's too rough for Lennox. Lennox is a gentleman, Golota is a brawler. He's an alley fighter. He'll do anything. You saw what happened to Golota.

"And he also felt threatened when he had a trainer that talked about him really bad named Don Turner, who said that Lennox was a coward. That all you had to do was back him up. He had a big, strong guy in Michael Grant. And you saw what happened to him at the end of the first round. They were dragging Grant back to his corner, picking him up off the floor. And you saw when Rahman dissed him real bad prior to the last fight. You saw what happened to Rahman. When Lennox Lewis feels threatened, that's when he's the most dangerous. And with Mike Tyson, we feel confident that Lennox feels threatened. And Mike Tyson is very much in danger of ending up going up out of that Pyramid point—or whatever it is up there—with a vicious upper-cut."

Then it was time for Lennox to rise and speak. There was a hushed, respectful silence, as Lewis would now talk publicly for the first time in almost a week. You felt a hint of tension and uneasiness in the air, as if the audience was a tad worried for him—that, God forbid, maybe the bad guy's intimidation tactics just might be working. There was a feeling of concern that Lewis could possibly be wilting under the pressure as the moment of truth neared.

But Lewis was not faltering. When the champion took his position at the podium, he radiated a supreme confidence that persuaded you he would be the victor come Saturday night. He thanked everyone for coming, appreciated the Memphis hospitality, promised a great fight and had no unkind words for Tyson. He also addressed Tyson's talkative trainers.

"Trainers don't do the fighting, [Tyson] does the fighting," said Lewis "His trainers can say all they want. They are trying to psyche him up and get him ready. They realize he likes that kind of talk. But if they want to talk like that, they need to remember—they aren't in the ring."

Lewis reiterated that he didn't fear Tyson, adding that "We both have a little fear in the sense that he fears me, and I do not want to lose."

He eloquently described the contrasting appeals of himself and Tyson.

"Some like those roughhouse tactics. They're excited

about it because they love train wrecks. And then there's the other person out there that loves the art of it, loves the sweet science of it. And those are the people who are attracted to me."

Afterwards, Steward had some more things to say. First, he debunked the Tyson camp accusations that Lewis was fearful of Tyson.

"This man has won an Olympic gold medal, a junior world championship. He's a three-time heavyweight champ, he's lost just twice and he knocked both fighters out in rematches," Steward said. "How is he going to let that little man run him around the ring? It's ridiculous.

"Lennox is very cool," Steward continued. "He is the one that made this fight. You don't make a fight against somebody you're afraid of. He went out of his way to make this fight."

Also, Steward said that Tyson bringing banned trainer Panama Lewis and Crocodile into camp earlier in the week was a sign in the Tyson camp that something was wrong. Panama Lewis once spent a year in jail after being convicted of removing the padding from Luis Resto's gloves the night he fought Irish Billy Collins in Madison Square Garden in 1983. Tyson invited Panama Lewis to be an "adviser." Because Panama Lewis's license was currently under suspension in New York—all states must honor that suspension according to the Federal Muhammad Ali Act—the disgraced trainer would not be permitted in Tyson's corner. But he is allowed to attend workouts and the fight.

"I think Mike is finally realizing what he's gotten himself into now," Steward said. "He wonders what he's doing fighting a guy this big. I think they've brought guys in to try and boost Mike's confidence."

Steward theorized what Tyson would do on Saturday night.

"Mike is a go-fast fighter like Joe Frazier, a head-forward, lunging, attack — when you just do it you don't think and you don't hesitate," he said. "Everything happens instinctively. As we all age more, we don't do things as instinctively. And we hesitate more. You can't fight the go, go, go fight. He'll fight that way for the first few rounds until he figures out that Lennox isn't a big, clumsy kid."

Steward said the whole world knows the strategy Lewis has to employ to tame Tyson.

"You have to pressure Mike the whole time, you have to make him fight," he said. "You can't let him attack, rest and then attack again. He was like that when I faced him when he was an amateur. You throw the left jab, you get physical when Mike gets close and hit him with right uppercuts when he gets frustrated. I'd like to see the fight end in two rounds. I think there's a chance of that happening."

Also on Wednesday, Tyson spoke, although it was only with four reporters, not the hundreds who had flocked to Memphis. One was Dan Rafael, then from *USA Today* and now of ESPN.com, and the other three were with the Memphis *Commercial-Appeal*. The four chosen journalists were invited to a session at a casino in Tunica, where Tyson talked to area children and answered their questions. Tyson appeared comfortable, relaxed, even jovial in the session, which was played on video in the media center.

The most interesting topic that Tyson discussed was about Cus D'Amato and how he had failed to heed the advice of his late mentor.

"Everything he told me, I never listened to," Tyson

admitted. "That's why I am in the situation I am in. But he always told me that your closest friends would betray you. People will want to be your friend because you're champion and because you're famous. People will write things about you. People are so fickle. They love you one minute and they hate you the next because they are unsure about their own destiny, which we all are.

"We don't know really what's going on here. We just go by what the Bible tells us or by what some philosopher tells us or the Koran or some religious book. We are all just followers trying to find the right place, but we don't know where the hell we are going. We're just going on doing it."

On Thursday, June 6, Tyson arrived for his weigh-in at the Pyramid. He was a perfect gentleman. There were seven officers assigned to protect him that afternoon. One of the patrolmen said of Tyson to the Memphis *Commercial-Appeal*, "He was the nicest fellow. He told me to call him Mike. It blew me away."

Another officer was equally impressed. "Mike is a down-to-earth, inner city kind of guy. If Mike had some positive people around him, he'd be a great guy."

Tyson hopped up on the scale wearing only white boxers, a white necklace and rapidly chewing a piece of gum. He weighed in at 234.5 while flexing his biceps and even smiling a bit. He looked impressive and ready. He wore an expression that conveyed that he would face his destiny with every ounce of defiance and gusto that he could possibly muster.

Tyson's trainer Ronnie Shields said that, right after the weigh-in, Tyson was going to "a Blockbuster and rent about fifteen movies. So I imagine he'll spend most of his time watching movies and thinking about the fight. He's calm and relaxed and in a great frame of mind."

Tyson gave an interview with ESPN's Jeremy Schaap while standing on the jam-packed crowded stage in his underwear.

"I'm in perfect shape. I just look forward to the fight. I trained hard, probably got a hundred-sixty rounds in for this particular fight. And I'm just looking forward for it to happen."

Tyson made reference to Steward's previous comments. "I was listening to Emanuel Lewis, Steward or whatever his name is, being a cheerleader. I'm from Bronxville, Brooklyn. I'm not afraid of nobody, in the ring or out of the ring, if they got a gun or a knife. And I'll show him that, too."

Schaap noticed Tyson was a bit jumpy and let Iron Mike know that he thought he seemed anxious.

"I'm just ready to get it on, to crush this guy's skull, show who the real world champion is. The best fighter of the era."

Schaap was courageous. He asked Tyson how he planned to "counter Lewis's height and reach advantages, which are significant."

Tyson didn't hesitate. "Listen. That's no significance in a man's character, his heart. That means nothing to me."

Schaap asked Tyson if he thought he was a better fighter now.

"Listen. Maybe I'm not as good of a fighter as I was fourteen years ago. But I'm sure he's not as good a fighter as he was fourteen years ago."

Tyson wasn't ducking any questions. He made eye contact. He looked good and sounded good. Next, he was asked about the fight's impact on his legacy.

"Listen. I already stamped my legacy on the immortal history of boxing. This is just another hurrah to add to it."

Was this fight any different from some of his other big fights? "It can't mean anything different, 'cause then it's something abnormal. Every fight is normal to me. Nothing is abnormal. This is just a fight, a party, so to speak."

Last, Tyson was asked what he would do in the last forty-eight hours.

"Just pray that he doesn't die of a heart attack," Tyson sneered with a sinister smile.

Lewis weighed in at 249.25. He raised his arms straight up, with his two index fingers indicating who was going to finish in first place on Saturday. He was the supreme ring gladiator of this generation, and he looked exactly like it.

"I'm definitely going to be popping out the jabs," he said after stepping off the scale. "If he gets by the jab, he's gonna run into my right hand. If he gets by my right hand, then he'll run into my uppercut."

I remember Lewis saying a few years earlier how important the jab was to his success.

"Jabs are the key to everything. They start off everything. Before you can do any combination, you jab first. The jab is a defensive weapon and an offensive weapon, and noted in history as being one of the prime weapons of the boxer. I can knock someone out if I catch them correctly. I can bloody his nose, get in the eyes. And I'm picking up points while I use it.

"You know, Muhammad Ali made the jab very famous. It's a weapon that's always in your face. It's my prime weapon, and when I don't use it, things seem to fall apart."

Two days before the fight, most of the Memphis hotels were booked solid. Sam's Town sold out all of its 850 rooms, charging $100 a room. The Sheraton Casino had no rooms available for the weekend, though Bally's and Grand Casino were still offering a place to stay for $249 a night, with a two-night minimum. Tickets were still available for the fight. Many were being advertised in the Memphis *Commercial-Appeal* for well under face value. Days before the fight, there were more than 150 ebay.com auctions offering fight tickets.

The impact of the Lewis-Tyson fight at the airports was massive. There were 170 additional flights scheduled for the weekend, according to the Federal Aviation Administration. Northwest Airlines officials said they were "treating the fight weekend as if it were a holiday like Thanksgiving or Christmas." Delta Airlines decided to use larger jets to fly into Memphis, and they were still overbooked. At West Memphis Airport, the staff worked twenty-four hours Friday, Saturday and Sunday. According to Linda Avery, the airport manager, she said Denzel Washington, Allen Iverson, Val Kilmer, the Dave Matthews Band and Wesley Snipes all arrived on private jets.

"Lewis-Tyson is the biggest promotion in the history of the sport," HBO executive Mark Taffet said. "When I say that, I mean that it is an event that has more awareness, more consumer marketing impressions and more anticipation than any other pay-per-view boxing event that has preceded it."

The world was converging on Memphis, Tennessee to witness this night of destiny.

X

Heavyweight Armageddon!

Things are not always as they seem.
Outward form deceives many. Rare is
the mind that discerns what is care-
fully concealed within.

— Phaedrus

No two men can be half an hour together, but one shall acquire an evident superiority over the other.

— Samuel Johnson

You must either conquer and rule or
serve and lose, suffer or triumph, be
the anvil or the hammer.

— Goethe

Nothing in the world compares to the excitement and
energy of a world heavyweight championship fight. Its
essence may have never been better described than by
Everett Skehan in his 1977 book *Rocky Marciano: Biography Of A First Son.*

"The crowning of a Heavyweight champion is a supreme occasion in sports. The fight that creates the new

king is important in its infinite detail. People who have no interest in boxing attend because it is the most chic place to be. For those who love the sport it is an eternal orgasm. Its celebration sizzles like a rare champagne that intoxicates the world. It is the ultimate in charisma, excitement, suspense. And nowhere is victory so consummately rewarding and defeat so inconsolably agonizing...In a world that claims to abhor violence and yet immerses itself in it, the Heavyweight champion is a symbol, the very image of power and survival. The toughest man alive. The most violent of the violent. An idol in a generation that no longer recognizes idols."

Mike Tyson was facing a double danger in Memphis. Not only was he about to compete against the best heavyweight in the world, he also cast himself in the role of the "bad guy." There are a lot more burdens and pressures that the "heel" has to deal with in his battle versus the good guy, the hero. I have heard this obscure boxing theory discussed very rarely. It was best explained by George Foreman.

The idea is about how public sentiment and favoritism can actually influence a boxing match, by subconsciously stripping the zap from the perceived bad guy's punch power. George Foreman is revered as one of the most popular, well-liked boxing champions of all-time, but his image today is a lot different than it was thirty years ago. Foreman in his prime was a misunderstood, bad guy-type champion with a sullen and introverted nature. Eventually, of course, he changed his attitude and public persona, and the public did warm to him but not until many years later.

Foreman talked about a conversation he once had with his one-time mentor and sparring partner, Sonny Liston. A runaway as a young boy in the South who later served time for armed robbery, Liston amazingly went on and succeeded by becoming the heavyweight champion in the 1960s. But Liston was a champion who never was accepted by the populace.

"When I won the championship from [Floyd] Patterson, everyone acted like I stole it," Liston told Foreman, who included the conversation in his autobiography *By George*. "What are you doing as Heavyweight champion? What's someone like you doing with the belt? When I was champ I used to hear people say I didn't deserve the title. Then when I lost to [Cassius] Clay, the same people told me I should have won. I know I should have won. I should have. I could have. But they acted like they didn't want me to."

Foreman wrote, "I interpreted Sonny's words as a sort of admission that he'd unconsciously sacrificed his title. To satisfy the fans who said he was unworthy or undeserving."

When Foreman lost to Ali in Africa, the same theory seemed to be at play. The entire continent seemed to be in favor of Ali. They even chanted in unison, *"Ali bomaye, Ali bomaye* (Ali kill him)!" All this united energy for Ali and against Foreman may have had a telepathic impact on the outcome of their historic match in 1974. Maybe Foreman did subliminally sacrifice his title to appease the will of the world. Or maybe Ali just could not have been beaten that night. It will always be an intriguing subject to ponder.

Now, Tyson was in the same position as Foreman and Liston—he was unquestionably representing the dark side. Here he was, a convicted rapist, a cannibalizing crazy man, fighting for the most prestigious prize in sport. He was barely fit to function in society, the moralists were saying. How could he possibly handle the immense responsibility of carrying the respected distinction as World Heavyweight Champion—the champion of the people?

"You're all a bunch of fuckin' assholes. You know why? You don't have the guts to be what you want to be. You need people like me. You need people like me so you can point you're fuckin' fingers. And say, That's the bad guy. So what's that make you? Good? You're not good. You just know how to hide. How to lie. Me? I don't have that problem. Me? I always tell the truth. Even when I lie. So say goodnight to the bad guy. Come on. The last time you're gonna see a bad guy like this again. Let me tell you. Come on. Make way for the bad guy."

This monologue was from the unforgettable restaurant scene of the film *Scarface*—Al Pacino as Tony Montana, who was nearing his demise. In a way, it reminds of Tyson, who also seemed to be headed to some sort of an end.

If the curtain, indeed, was ready to fall on Tyson's career, many respectable experts disagreed. There was still a loyal contingent of those who faithfully believed in Tyson as a fighter. Oliver McCall was one. He was Tyson's former sparring partner and the first man to defeat Lewis.

"There are two things that Lennox does that Mike will take advantage of," McCall predicted. "First, he paws with his jab. Tyson will do just like he did to Carl 'The Truth' Williams. He slipped and threw a vicious left hook and the fight was over. The second thing Lennox does is telegraph the right hand. Tyson will catch him."

Holyfield was still criticizing Lewis by saying he had

"...more respect for Tyson"—a man he has beaten twice—than for Lewis, who he claims is "not prepared to lay it all on the line like great champions should." Holyfield continued with his assertion Tyson would win. "I don't think anybody is going to beat Tyson going backwards. Tyson may not be as strong as Lewis, but he's very explosive. Tyson is very quick, and when he hits a guy, the impact of the quickness gets you off your feet. What scares people is they don't see it."

Former Cruiserweight Champ Bobby Czyz was giving the nod to Tyson. "Listen. Not just because I like Mike and we're friendly. But I think Mike's gonna win the fight, because he's the better all-around fighter. Lennox Lewis has shown he's a great boxer, but not very durable. And Mike hits as hard as it gets. I think Mike will wear him down by the eighth round."

Czyz once told me a very touching personal story about how he became friends with Tyson.

"I'll show you his human side. May, nineteen-eighty-seven. I was doing the Roy Firestone show, *Up Close on ESPN*. Right before, Mike Tyson was fighting Pinklon Thomas for the heavyweight title, defending his title. I did the show. I was very vulnerable and opened myself up to the public and let them know about my tragic childhood.[10] When I flew into Vegas with my friends to watch the fight—Mike won the fight, won every round—after the fight I went over and gave him a big hug, gave him a kiss, said, Hey how you doing Mike? He goes, Hey, Bobby, I cried. I say, Why? You killed the

---

[10] Czyz's father committed suicide in the living room of the family house

guy.[11] He said, No. I saw your interview with Roy Firestone. It brought me to tears."

Earnie Shavers, who still holds the highest knockout percentage in heavyweight history: "Lewis will beat Tyson. Tyson is over the hill, and he has no heart. Lewis will intimidate him and put pressure on him. Tyson's made for him. Lennox Lewis is without a doubt the true champion. But I think, until he beats Tyson, he will never get the recognition he wants."

HBO's Larry Merchant expected Lewis to emerge the winner. But he wasn't so sure. "Mike Tyson winning the heavyweight title would be the worst scenario for boxing. But the truth of the matter is that, in boxing, the worst things often occur."

Hasim Rahman, the other man to defeat Lewis, had an interesting opinion on the fight. "I like Lennox to win. His footwork is excellent. In our second fight, I couldn't reach him, I couldn't get into range. I barely touched him. And Tyson's a lot smaller[12] than me."

Former Light Heavyweight Champ Jose Torres noted, "When an intimidator fails to intimidate, he becomes intimidated. What separates a champion from an ordinary fighter is character."

Lou DiBella, the astute boxing promoter, simply said, "I think Tyson gets the shit kicked out of him."

Greg Juckett, then the editor of *Boxing Digest* and now with www.secondsout.com, wondered how some observers sensed fear inside of Lewis. "It's really surprising to me that there are people who actually believe

---

[11] Tyson stopped Thomas in the 6th round

[12] nearly four inches

Lewis is scared of Tyson. Lewis isn't scared of anyone. No one."

Showtime commentator Al Bernstein, one of the shrewdest of the veteran boxing pundits, was impressed by Lewis's composure. "Lennox Lewis is a man who is calm, who never approaches fights in a different way. Lennox Lewis is a man who when you see him in these big fight situations, you pretty much always see the same demeanor. For one simple reason...I think the word 'unflappable' describes him better than any athlete I've ever seen. And because of that I constantly feel confident that he'll give a great effort in the ring.

"I find Lennox to be a refreshing heavyweight champion. He is very intelligent and well-spoken. And he's a big puncher who's mostly scored knockouts. He's a lethal puncher. But his demeanor in the ring and outside the ring doesn't make you believe he's doing it with the ferocity that he is. As a pure, right-handed puncher, he's one of the best the sport has ever seen. When he's focused—and he looks extremely focused to me—he gets the job done. And that's the bottom line."

Kevin Rooney, Tyson's trainer until being fired in 1988, thought his old charge had a good chance. "Hey, if Mike hits him on the chin, he's going to go," Rooney said. "But it doesn't matter, because these guys are in their mid-thirties and there isn't a lot left in the heavyweight division. That's why Lewis and Tyson and Holyfield are still there, because there is so little talent out there.

"Since he left us, Mike has been on a fast track to hell, in terms of his boxing. I haven't spoken to him for a long time, but I don't hold any animosity toward him or hate him. I still care about him. But it makes me sick to think of all he threw away. I could throw up when I really think about it. It's sad. It's just sad.

"The thing that bothers me is that he could have been the greatest heavyweight ever. After he beat Spinks, I started telling him we had to think about breaking Rocky Marciano's [unbeaten 49-0] record. Hell, he could have gone a hundred-zero. I tried to say something to keep him interested, to keep him motivated. Because after he did what he did to Spinks, he was head and shoulders above everyone else. It wasn't close. He easily could have gone sixty-zero, seventy-zero, with no problems. Don King ruined the guy."

Kevin Rooney would not be in Memphis. He would watch the fight at his home in Catskill, NY.

Frans Botha, who lost by knockout to both Lewis and Tyson, liked Lewis's chances better. "Lewis has to watch out early. But Lewis can do a number on him. If he gets through the first round, Lewis wins."

Glyn Leach, editor of *British Boxing Monthly* magazine, was another who was still a believer in Tyson. "Lewis should win because he has every physical advantage. *Should* win. But the more I think about it, the more I think Tyson will stop him. You can't tell me Tyson won't land one hard punch. And that's all it can take. I think it is better for boxing if Tyson wins. And I think he might just do that in spectacular fashion."

Arnie Boehm, Lewis' first coach, said, "Lennox has a great chance to win. But I will be very nervous for him." Boehm would be there at ringside. Lewis made sure Boehm was always there for his title fights. Boehm always received first-class airline tickets and a limousine to pick him up. The champion remembered where he came from.

Teddy Atlas gave his typically intriguing synopsis of the fight. "There is no doubt that Mike Tyson is very insecure. The opposite of how he tries to act inside the ring, how he talks. He only knows how to be what he's been. Which is a guy that's really tormented, tortured. He is not at all sure of himself. He is trying to keep the wolves from the door. Which is to hide how he really feels. Which is absolutely zero about himself.

"When you live the wrong way and you don't feel good about yourself, how are you going to get into that squared circle? How are you going to find the place to summon the strength to step on some kind of plateau where you can feel like you can stand up to another man? You can't."

Betting odds were swaying late, leaning towards a Tyson victory. British bookmaker William Hill cut the odds on Tyson winning from 13-8 to 11-8. And raised Lewis from 4-9 to 8-15.

"The betting has been one way traffic," A William Hill spokesman said. "And at the moment, Tyson winning would be a six-figure loss for us."

In Las Vegas, Lewis closed as the -200 favorite. But he had opened at -250. The majority of Las Vegas sports books saw heavy Tyson action. The "smart" money was going for a Tyson win.

Chris Eubank, the eccentric former WBO Super Middleweight ruler, had an original take on the fight. "Hatred is the wrong word [to describe how Lewis and Tyson feel about each other]. They have been in love with each other for six months. Being in love is thinking about the person ninety percent of their days. They're consumed with each other. That's all they've been doing.

"All hell's gonna break loose. If Lewis stands his

ground, the fight goes in favor of Tyson. Tyson will put pressure on Lewis like you've never seen, like anyone's put pressure on anyone before. It's going to be complete magic."

It promised to be the classic battle of good versus evil, light vs. dark, power vs. power. The reserved and private champion vs. the outspoken menace to society. The well-mannered impeccable sportsman vs. the spontaneously combustible barbarian. The tall, elegant boxer vs. the blocky brute brawler. Refined skill vs. savage blockbuster.

Much of the world was captivated by Lewis-Tyson. but a superfight is only a superfight if it can attract an abundance of celebrities. And the celebrities were coming in droves to illuminate Memphis. Adding spice to the ringside atmosphere inside the Pyramid were to be the likes Donald Trump, Morgan Freeman, Isaac Hayes, Ashanti, Cuba Gooding Jr., Denzel Washington, Samuel L. Jackson, David Hasselhoff, The Rock, Warren Zevon, Jermaine O'Neal, Steve McNair, Tim Watters, members of the metal band Saliva, Halle Berry, LL Cool J, Leonardo DiCaprio, Roy Jones Jr., Holyfield, Sugar Ray Leonard, Thomas Hearns, Jay-Z and Heidi Fleiss.

Since the beginning, prizefighting has always attracted popular celebrities and renowned artists. The Jack Dempsey-Gene Tunney rematch lured Somerset Maugham, Walter Chrysler, Charles Schwab and Al Capone to Chicago's Soldier Field. William Thackeray and Charles Dickens went to Farnborough, England, in 1860 to watch Tom Sayers fight John Heenan. Over the last century, the notable ringsiders range from Boris Karloff, Brad Pitt, Pam Anderson and Pete Sampras to Ernest Hemingway, William Randolph Hearst, Franklin Delano Roosevelt and Oprah Winfrey.

Just before departing for the arena from his rented house, Lewis was studying a videotape of Tyson's first defeat of Buster Douglas. His final preparations in the last twenty-four hours before battle were quite interesting and rather unique.

"Just before we left to go to the arena, we turned Douglas-Tyson on," Courtney Shand said. "He watched that tape a lot in that house."

I asked Shand what they did in the last forty-eight hours before the fight, to prime Lewis to be at his optimum peak, mentally and physically. "There's a lot of dead time, with idle time on your hands. That's where the mental focus has to be real sharp. There's enough to stimulate you. But you can get bored. And if you start getting bored, sitting there trying to not think about the fight, trying to put your mind in other places, that can be catastrophic.

"So, our main focus on that day before and during the fight is certain points, certain things. We might see him get up and do something. When he does it, you remind him of certain things. If he gets up and starts moving around, okay, remember when you do that? Do this. And as soon as you do that, do that. Positive reinforcement. If you push Tyson a certain way, we know what he's going to do before he resets himself to throw a punch. So, capitalize on that. When Mike does things a certain way, expect this. Positive reinforcing. We don't just go in and jump on him. As soon as Lennox shows us that fire, we're on him. Keep drilling it in. Keep drilling it in."

"Again, its when he gets up and turns on the TV, he watches a certain section of the fight, okay, remember do this when you see this. What do you do if…? Sometimes we put questions on him. Okay, you saw what Buster just did right there, okay, what do you gotta do when that happens? When you get him off you, what do you have to do? Just keeping his mind stimulated.

"'Cause he has to read it. 'Cause he's like a quarterback in a football game. He gets up there, he sees the defense lining up, just before he huts the ball and they shift—he's got to read that. It's the same thing. He's got to read what Tyson is gonna do. Read from his body language. Read from the way he's setting his feet. Because Tyson's, like, a deliberate fighter.

"We watch our fights, too. Because we gotta analyze what the other guy is trying to analyze about us. See what things we're doing that they might try to take advantage of. They're smart, and we think we're smart. They're trying to match wits."

"By the time he goes to bed, God bless his sleeping. He does sleep. But I don't personally think he can sleep on Saturday because of all that reinforcement, all the stuff we've worked on the week before the fight. It's a dangerous time. Because all that week you go from training six, seven hours a day to the week of the fight, training maybe an hour, an hour-and-twenty minutes the whole day. There's a lot of dead time that we need to keep him focused."

Shand says Lewis also likes to watch karate movies and play table tennis in those final hours. Lewis says table tennis sharpens his hand and eye speed.

As the team gathered to leave the house for the Pyramid, Lewis showed his sense of humor when it was least expected. "He said, 'Call HBO, tell them I'm not fighting. Tell them the fight's off,'" said Scott DeMercardo. Then Lewis smiled and the small entourage climbed into a white Ford Explorer stretch limousine.

Lewis emerged from the vehicle inside the Pyramid looking perfectly relaxed. HBO cameramen were there to greet him. He was wearing a red sweatsuit, black ragamuffin hat and black shades. He was chewing gum. Tyson arrived just before Lewis in a giant Rolls Royce limo wearing a tight-fitting blue short-sleeved muscle shirt. He was looking cool, too, except for the huge sweatstains on his shirt.

They went straight to their respective dressing rooms. Lewis prefers a quiet dressing room so he can stretch out on a cot and catch a snooze. It's hard to believe that a man could manage to take a nap with such a daunting task so near, but Lewis likes to sleep a little before stretching and getting his hands wrapped.

Tyson, by contrast, takes the more expected approach to fight preparation. In fact, it was once reported, before the Tyson-Spinks fight, he punched holes in the concrete wall while rousing himself into a rage. You could imagine the high-voltage mood in Tyson's room, with Crocodile hollering and the rap music blaring.

After the final preliminary — IBF Junior Featherweight Champ Manny Pacquiao crushed Jorge Julio in the second round — the moment of truth had finally arrived. The ring was empty for a good thirty minutes as everyone waited for the warriors to arrive.

Then Mike Tyson strode out of his dressing room, to the beat of rap music by DMX's "What's My Name?". Iron Mike had his gloves together in front of his heart, with the customary white towel covering his body. At first glance, he looked slightly apprehensive, even reluctant for the fight, in contrast to how he seemed at the weigh-in. His posture looked a bit slumpy and droopy. He banged his hands together a few times as he neared the ring.

The entire crowd was mesmerized by the appearance of Tyson, one of the mightiest, most notorious and celebrated fighters the world had ever witnessed, but the fire was not burning at full intensity. To my eyes, he looked like he was there more because he had to be than because he wanted to be. That's how he appeared. There was a subdued element to his mood.

When Iron Mike stepped through the ropes wearing his black trunks and black boots with no socks, much of the crowd applauded him. Love him or hate him, this was a man who defied all odds and achieved unparalleled greatness and distinction in the brutal sport of boxing. Upon hearing the acclaim, Tyson looked around, slightly inquisitive, acknowledging the unexpected warm greeting. He raised his arms about halfway—not all the way up—in a muted pose of triumph. He looked a little nervous, even uncomfortable. But it was still Mike Tyson. Iron Mike Tyson was in the ring.

Lewis came into sight from behind his dressing room door. He was robeless as well, and his standard reggae ring-entrance music of Bob Marley's "Crazy Bald Heads" was a perfect choice for the mood—his mood. Lewis looked fascinatingly calm. His body language was erect and lucid. He looked primed. His expression was stoic and focused, seemingly totally unaffected by any feelings of fright, apprehension or pressure. He looked like the winner was supposed to look.

Lewis exuded a mastery of control, like he had reached a higher plateau. It looked as if just one thing was on his mind, with every brain cell working in unison to serve just one single purpose—conquering and destroying Mike Tyson. Incredible—it truly is—how a man can keep himself so composed and so relaxed in such a moment of high stress. Here he is, about to engage in a fistfight in front of millions, perhaps billions. Yet there is not a single signal of any external discomfort.

I've always marveled at the disposition of a great fighter just before he is to do battle. It is one of the most awesome displays of humanity — man at his physical best. There are a great number of self-made millionaires, talented artists and renowned doctors and scientists, but there is only one Heavyweight Champion of the World. Capturing the heavyweight title is one of the most difficult tasks on earth. Maybe even the most difficult endeavor a man can do. As former champ Hasim "The Rock" Rahman so eloquently said after winning the title, "Most boxers are not perceived as terribly bright. But nobody playing one game of basketball or one game of golf can make twenty or thirty million dollars. I can fight for one second and make thirty million dollars. Why isn't everyone boxing?"

When Lewis stepped into the ring, he looked more than ready, like it was the place in the world he most wanted to be. He hopped a few steps, looked around briefly, gave a slight nod to his supporters, then settled about a yard from ring center, gazing over at Tyson.

There was no doubt about it, Lewis was the predator. There was a twelve-man wall of security dividing the ring, all attired in yellow shirts and black pants. Lewis's eyes looked clear and clean and spirited. You could detect not even an iota of doubt in his disposition.

"Tyson came up to the barrier," Lewis would say later. "Looking at me, looking at my body. I'm beating my stomach. Yeah, I'm ready."

As Lewis focused his sights on the target, ring announcer Jimmy Lennon began the introductions.

"A very good evening, ladies and gentlemen, and welcome to the Pyramid."

The crowd was enthralled. There is no more exciting moment in sports than the final moments before a super-fight.

"It is time for our historic night of boxing and our long-awaited and much anticipated featured bout of the evening."

Intro maestro extraordinaire Michael Buffer was also there to contribute his touch of class to the grand event.

"Tonight, here in Tennessee, we will turn the page to another chapter in the history book of boxing legends. Ladies and gentleman, this is the main event. Twelve rounds of boxing for the linear, legitimate and the universally recognized, undisputed heavyweight championship of the *woooorld*!"

Tyson had his mouthpiece in already and was staring back at Lewis while stepping softly in place. He looked not at all like the man who once said he wanted "to smear the champion's pompous brains all over the canvas." Or that he would "put a bullet in the back of the motherfucker's neck if he ever tried to intimidate me again."

Tyson and Lewis were still locked in eye contact. Lewis looked like a man in a perfect state of relaxation. Tyson looked not nearly as confident, even vulnerable. He could not break that awesome expression of calm Lewis wore.

"It's the time we've all been waiting for," Lennon continued. "Live from the Pyramid in Memphis, it's *fight time*!"

Lewis broke his stance and paced around a little, as if to huddle with himself, to digest what he had just seen in Tyson's eyes. Tyson followed that idea and also re-treated. He walked back to his corner, where he threw a couple of practice punches.

Lewis quickly regained his position and again began studying Tyson from near the center of the ring.

"Introducing to you first, the challenger, to my right," went Lennon. "He is fighting out of the blue corner, entering the ring wearing his traditional solid black trunks. From Catskill, New York, he weighed in at two hundred-thirty-four and a half pounds, with a record of forty-nine wins, three losses, two no-contests. He has forty-three big wins coming by knockout. Here he is, the youngest man ever to win the heavyweight title, currently ranked the number-one contender by the WBC. Please welcome the challenger, two-time Heavyweight Champion of the World...introducing the one and only ...Iron...Mike... *Tyson*!"

There was enormous applause and respect given to Tyson as the bell was rung six times during the uproar. He was pacing now. He banged his gloves together then put them up to his chin in his defensive guard. When Lennon announced his name, Iron Mike bowed three times then walked around some more, looking down mostly. He did not look over at Lewis. He seemed, to an observer, to reveal tiny hints of regret, shame and doubt in his body language. I really think I saw those feelings in his expression.

"And fighting out of the red corner..." Buffer kept it going. "...wearing white trimmed with red letters and officially weighing two hundred forty-nine and a quar-ter pounds. He captured Olympic gold in nineteen-eighty-eight. Now, as a professional, he has thirty-nine victories, including thirty KOs and three world titles. He has two defeats and a draw, all by way of rematch and then changed to victory, making him one of the few men in boxing history to have virtually defeated every man he has ever faced.

"Ladies and gentlemen, from London, England, presenting the three-time world champion, the linear, legitimate, universally recognized, undisputed Heavyweight Champion of the World, *Lennox Lewis!*"

Lewis never took his eyes off Tyson. Focused as could be, he raised his hands all the way up, never changing that supremely confident facial expression. My goodness, how he was able to maintain it was impressive in itself. The crowd was in pandemonium as it chanted, "Lewis! Lewis! Lewis!"

There were no traditional ring instructions—Referee Eddie Cotton had delivered them in the dressing rooms about an hour earlier. Both men went to their corners as the security men exited the combat zone in single file.

Tyson was all alone on his side of the ring. His trainers seemed to depart rather quickly. He stood there facing his corner, saying some kind of prayer, or so it looked like. Lewis stood with Steward and Knight, still studying Tyson.

Then Buffer bellowed his world-famous sentence.

"There's only one thing left to say. Let's get ready to *rumbuuuuull!*"

∞ Round One ∞

At the bell, the adrenaline levels in the building could have launched a rocket. Lewis came out quicker, more aggressively. Tyson did not come barreling out as expected. He waited to see what Lewis would do. Tyson threw the first two punches, two jabs. Lewis responded with two missed jabs.

The Pyramid was in a frenzy. Both battlers were

tuned in now. The first power punch was a Tyson right that fell way short, but it looked frightening, even if it missed the mark. Then Lewis landed a big right uppercut. Lewis thought it connected well enough to follow up, because Tyson almost staggered away off-balance. He landed a couple of bombs but not on the chin, as Tyson was on the ropes.

Tyson grabbed hold, and Lewis tried another uppercut. The big bombers were bombing away now!

But they weren't landing on target. Yet. There were many clinches. Both boxers were balancing their attacks with some caution. Though Lewis had six inches in height on Tyson, somehow it didn't look so. Yes, indeed, Tyson had a presence larger than life.

Tyson landed a left hook to the jaw, but Lewis was unfazed by it. Lewis kept sneaking in those big right uppercuts. Neither warrior would back up. Both were asserting by coming forward. At the bell, both took an extra look at each other, but that was it.

"In the first round, I was, like, I'm not gonna give up my ground," Lewis said afterwards. "I'm the champion."

Steward told Lewis, "Just settle down. If you know how bad he looks, it would be surprising. Settle down, get yourself together, start working your jab. You took all that anger, you're already slowing him down by wrestling him down and tying him up. Just take your time. Don't make the fight he's trying to make you fight. Just take your time, work the jab and hit him with the right hand and the uppercut."

Shields told Tyson, "One, two. But don't let this guy tire you out. Just relax yourself, baby. You had a good round. You won the first round. Try to come up top first, then the uppercut, okay? Be fast, baby, be fast."

Tyson won the first round on all three scorecards, 10-9.

∞◌∞

Tim Smith (Columnist for *The New York Daily News*): "We were in Louisville. And we see this guy coming out of the hotel. And we come out of the hotel, and we see this guy and he's got like a million tattoos. And he's a Brit. So we were talking to him. He's got, like, a tattoo [of Tyson] on his back, like, a full portrait; he's got the record up and down each arm, and it's incredible.

"We ask the guy, Why do you have all this stuff, these tattoos of Tyson? It's never gonna go away. And he's, like, I love the guy that much that I'm gonna die with all this stuff on my body, with Tyson on my body. And he says that he never misses an opportunity to come to see Tyson fight, whether he's in America or whether it's in London."

You witnessed Tyson with this man? "Yeah, Tyson actually came up and talked with the guy, and he was, like, admiring the artwork on his back and how real it was. Tyson thought it was cool that somebody would actually immortalize him on their body. Tyson loved it. He thought it was unbelievable. I thought it was unbelievable. It was in Louisville at the hotel lobby. The guy was from Manchester, I think."

∞ Round Two ∞

They settled into a clinch without a punch being thrown. Cotton warned only Lewis for holding. A roar of boos rebuked him for his over-officiating.

Lewis now was beginning to establish his rhythm and range, popping quick jabs with some uppercuts mixed in. You could see he was overpowering Tyson

148

now with pushes and shoves. Cotton warned Lewis a second time for holding, but it seemed Tyson was just as guilty of that infraction.

The pace slowed considerably. The Lewis jabs and uppercuts began to flow. Tyson had no answers to get inside. Lewis's size and footwork kept Tyson on the outside.

The champion's footwork is an art in itself. It is a skill he works very hard on. Prior to the Botha fight, on the last day of training camp, Lewis voiced his intent to play tennis. Tennis, he believed, sharpened his footwork. Everyone objected, worrying about some kind of ankle injury that could postpone the fight. But the champ calls the shots, and so it was tennis they played. Lewis's footwork was so masterful for that fight, I don't think he got hit with a single punch from Botha in that four-minute mismatch.

Lewis was in control now. He punctuated his round with another jolting right uppercut, right at the bell. In his corner, Tyson had his head down as Shields spoke. "Okay, champion, look. Listen to me. I told you, you cannot let this man poke too many jabs at you without you coming back with something."

Tyson nodded, looking guilty. "Right."

"Okay, you started using your face, but you quit jabbing. You have to be in this man's chest, you understand? Make this a very ugly fight now."

Steward told Lewis, "He's slowing down real bad. Work the jab. The jab is pumping. You're on your way. You're on your way, baby."

All three judges had Lewis, 10-9.

Thomas Hauser (Award-winning journalist, excerpt from an article that appeared in *The Observer Sports*

Monthly and his book *Chaos, Corruption, Courage and Glory*, published in 2005 by Sports Media Publishing Inc.):

"I learned to play chess in Canada, in public school when I was fifteen years old," Lennox told me. "And over time, my game improved because of boxing. I had a trainer in the amateurs named Adrian Teodorescu. He took me on trips to boxing tournaments and we'd play chess to pass the time. Adrian was quite good. Now I play as often as I can."

But only against people.

"I don't like playing against computers," Lennox continued. "You can't distract a computer, and a computer doesn't make mistakes. A lot of this game is psychological, and it's impossible to get inside a computer's head."

Last year, Lewis played more than a hundred games of chess.

"Many of them were in training camp," he reminisced. "With side bets for push-ups against friends who felt that their skills were superior to mine."

"I honestly don't like him playing chess," Lennox's trainer, Emanuel Steward, had said at the time. "I see him sitting there for ten minutes, thinking four moves ahead before he makes one. And he actually does the same thing in the ring — he thinks too much."

"I disagree with Emanuel," Lennox said prior to our own game. "The thought processes of chess are similar to boxing. You look at an opponent and what he does and then you devise a strategy to beat him."

"Chess has been here for a thousand years," Lennox continued. "It's a game for thinkers, and there's a lot of strategy involved. Chess shows the power of the mind, it opens different doors in the mind; and without it, I might not use that part of my mind. Those things appeal to me. It's one of the reasons I'm teaching my fiancée how to play chess. She's just starting to learn now how the pieces move."

"How good are you?" I queried.

"Not bad. I haven't taken it seriously to the point of trying to become ranked. I use it purely for recreation. But I don't just play chess. I'm a chess player."

The first few moves of our competition were a feeling-out process as Lennox satisfied himself that he wasn't sitting across the board from a ringer. In chess, as in boxing, one mistake can turn the competition around in a hurry. Lose a key exchange early, and it's like fighting with blood dripping into your eye for the entire the night.

Six moves into our game, Lennox took one of my knights at the cost of a mere pawn. The exchange reminded me of how Muhammad Ali used to go into a clinch early in a fight to test his opponent's physical strength. When Ali fought Jean-Pierre Coopman in 1976, they clinched in the first minute and Muhammad came out of the clinch laughing. Then, after the first round, he leaned over the ring ropes and shouted down at a network television executive, "You guys are in trouble. Ain't no way you're gonna get all your commercials in."

The tone for Lewis versus Hauser was now set. Lennox attacking, me on the defensive, throwing an occasional punch, trying to land something but expecting to be knocked out.

I moved my queen to the middle of the board in the hope of establishing an offensive.

"Interesting," Lennox commented.

Then I brought my remaining knight into play.

"Not bad," Lennox noted.

And then something marvelous happened. The chess board began to look more even to me.

"Nice move," Lennox complimented. "Very good…"

We traded pawns twice, and I exchanged a rook for a Lennox Lewis bishop and knight. Now I felt like a club fighter who thinks that maybe he has a chance to beat the champion after all.

"Who do you think Wladimir Klitschko should fight after Lamon Brewster?" Lennox queried.

"You're trying to distract me."

Whack ! My queen went down.

Then Lennox started reading a newspaper between moves, which is the equivalent of a fighter eating Chinese food between rounds.

The outcome was no longer in doubt.

There are no decisions in chess, only knockouts and draws. This one had all the makings of a knockout. If our chess game had been a fight, the referee would have stepped in and stopped it at that point.

Lennox's queen was in my face like a poleaxing jab. Next, the heavy right hands started landing. In truth, I was obliterated. But like a fighter, I went out on my shield.

Forty minutes after we'd begun, Lennox leaned forward in his chair and smiled. "Checkmate," he said.

∞ Round Three ∞

Lewis continued the pattern of controlling the range with jabs and right hands. Lewis's graceful movements conjured the image of a great artist at work, poetically using his fists as tools to sculpt defeat onto this hulking shape of clay. Tyson's only answers were one-punch-at-a-time attacks, which Lewis easily thwarted. The size and reach disadvantages were just too much for Tyson.

Lewis drew first blood—a small cut over Tyson's right eye. Tyson looked to be in pain as Shields implored him, "You got to get closer to this man."

But no man in fifteen years had ever really done so. Those Lewis jabs and rights were a mighty and dangerous arsenal to penetrate. Tyson grimaced as his cutman, Ira Trocki, tended to the wound.

Steward told Lewis, "He can't deal with your uppercut. Let's get it together. The man is tired."

Lewis won on all three judges' scorecards, 10-9.

"T" Warren (Brooklyn resident):

I hung out with Mike Tyson on numerous occasions. He's a beautiful man, a beautiful individual. I know the real Mike, you know what I'm saying? He's honest, he's a decent, lovable man. Not what the media makes him up to be. A big, you know, crazy, you know. He's a beautiful, beautiful man.

Any lasting memory come to mind? It's a whole lot of them. I can't just explain one...when we're riding our bikes. When he comes to Brownsville, and we're riding the motorcycles all around Brownsville, you know, everywhere, Bed-Stuy, Crown Heights, just enjoying life.

How many of you guys? It's a whole lot. Once they see two, three, it becomes fifty, sixty, seventy, eighty bikes, you know? Yeah, that's how it go. Everyone knows when Mike is in the neighborhood. He makes his stops where he normally used to be at. He makes his pitstops.

Eighty bikes? Where do you end up at? We might go to a

Rucker [basketball league] game on 140th St. up-town—havin' a beautiful of a time.

What kind of bike does Mike have? He rides a Harley in the summertime. Or a three-wheeler. Mike has the little bucket helmet on, you know, the bikin' helmet. You can see his face. Everyone knows him, man. Especially in Brownsville. Sometimes, he comes back for softball games on Sundays, and back-catch for us, play first base, hit. Yeah, that's Mike, beautiful individual.

∞ Round Four ∞

It was evident now that Lewis was in the process of demonstrating another classic exhibition of the sweet science. Out in Las Vegas, Muhammad Ali was watching the fight with LeRoy Neiman at a private screening at the Paris Hotel. The two were together for a co-signing.

"At the start of the fight, Ali was very stoic," Neiman told me. "He'd settle back between rounds. A few people would come up to him between rounds, and he'd nod and sign some things. Then, when the round started again, he'd be absolutely riveted to the screen.

"As Lewis got his rhythm going, Ali picked up on that. It reached him. Then he'd start throwing these little punches in his seat. He was fighting like Lewis in there, leaning back in his seat, bobbing and weaving. Ali had that reaction to it. He likes fast, clean, effective punches. There was no question Lewis was going to win it."

The Brits in the Pyramid were chanting again, this time with even more energy and emphasis.

"*Lewis! Lewis! Lewis!*" Lewis looked like a scientist, picking apart and dissecting Tyson with lefts and rights from all kinds of different angles.

Suddenly, Lewis landed three jabs. And then a thudding right froze Tyson, who fell on his back after a slight push from Lewis. He lay there, hurt.

But Cotton ruled that it wasn't a knockdown! He even took a point from Lewis for pushing. Eddie Cotton's actions in the ring this night were, to put it mildly, quite suspicious.

Then the bell rang.

Steward was now frantic, but for another reason. He wanted Lewis to attack more forcefully.

"Step it up, man. This man is finished. You got this man, and you're like this [He tapped Lewis lightly on the chest]. Step on it and turn into it. Or you might get caught with some crazy shit."

Shields said, "You can't just run in. The right hand is down. When he jabs, throw the right hand."

Cotton's point deduction on Lewis made it a 9-9 round for all three judges.

T.J. Moses (Brooklyn resident):

I remember one summer about six, seven years ago, Tyson rolled up. He used to ride his Harley around Brooklyn. And he was riding around. And some of me and my people were outside, on Crown Street. And a couple of me and my boys was slap boxing, just playin' around. Tyson rolled up. By himself. And everybody looked. They were wondering if that was Tyson or not.

So, he just rolls up and he say, Yo. I'll give whoever knocks the other one out, I'll give you one hundred dollars right now.

So, that just got people hyped. Word! Word! So they just started rumblin', rumblin', rumblin'. Next thing you know my boy just catches him with two lefts and a right—boop, boop…boop—and he just dropped. Boop. Tyson said, Good shit. Gave him a hundred dollars, got on his bike and left. I said, Oooohh, shit. I say, Yo, that's too much power for one man to have. It was like straight out of a movie scene. Because we just chillin'. He just comes out of nowhere.

∞ Round Five ∞

Tyson looked worn out, battered. Lewis maintained his dominance. Cotton warned Lewis again for holding. It again seemed unwarranted, like maybe Cotton had it in for Lennox.

Steward was near panic. "Just let that shit go. This fight is over. You're gonna let that man get you with some shit if you don't watch. That man is dead over there. He wants to quit. Right hand over the top. This man is dangerous. You've got to get him out of here."

Lewis kept his cool, as always, eyeing over Tyson's way as if to measure how near he was to completing his masterpiece.

Tyson had cuts over both eyes, and his nose was bleeding. He looked beaten. Like a man who was accepting his punishment from Lewis, like a man who realized he deserved this beating for all the foul behavior over the last few years. Tyson was enduring his whupping with a remarkable dignity, like most of the great champions inevitably do. A champion in victory and a champion in defeat.

Lewis won 10-9 on all three cards.

∞∞

Sechew Powell (Junior middleweight contender from Brooklyn):

"I saw Mike Tyson the night he beat Michael Spinks in Atlantic City. And he came through the neighborhood, and he had the belts on. He stuck his head out the sunroof. And it was exciting for everybody in the neighborhood, for all the kids, everybody.

It was pretty late at night. So, my mother let me come outside and take a look at the excitement going on outside. It was exciting. The night he beat Spinks, he came back. He had family across the street, so he was checkin' his aunts out and his family, showin' them some love. And in the process, he ended up showing the whole neighborhood some love, you know.

I remember it was a white limo. He stuck his head out the sunroof. And he had the belts crisscrossed the way he used to wear 'em, and it was a big moment for everybody in the neighborhood, to get that close to someone who was a celebrity.

He just posed. They were cheering, yelling, congratulating Mike. That's the way to go, Mike! Saying things you would say if you saw a hero of yours.

∞ **Round Six** ∞

Tyson threw some shots but none were close to the target. Lewis was much more accurate. He was simply pulverizing Tyson now. The ring general in charge. Effective aggression. Totally in control. Like the big cat playing with, almost torturing his mouse.

But Tyson was game, so game. No one can ever say Iron Mike doesn't have heart. Look where his heart took him to—all the way from the Brooklyn ghetto to center stage of the biggest prizefight in boxing history.

10-9, Lewis.

Eric Bottjer (Matchmaker):

I met Lennox Lewis in 1990 at a show at the Washington D.C. Convention Center. I was talking with Ollie Dunlap, who was involved with Lewis at the beginning of his pro career, and then Lewis walked up. Nobody recognized him at the time. Ollie's introduction was, "Do you know who this is." I did, and I just blurted out to Lewis, "What the hell are you doing around here?"

He just smiled. "I'm incognito," he replied. We talked for a few moments and then separated to go watch the fights.

About eight months later, I was in Norfolk at the Pernel Whitaker-Poli Diaz fight when I saw Lewis in a hotel lobby. He came up to me and, calling me by my name, asked how I was doing. I was amazed, one, that he would even remember meeting me, and two, that he would remember my name and seem to have a sincere interest in my well-being. Later that night at the fights, as the Michael Moorer-Alex Stewart fight was starting, he asked me my opinion on the outcome. He struck me as very thoughtful and very real.

He also had a nice-looking woman with him. It always humored me, these rumors of Lewis being gay, because whenever I saw him afterward, more often than not he was with a female friend. This was before he became famous in the US, so I don't think it was for show. At one HBO party he had an absolute knockout literally leading him around by one of his dreadlocks. I thought to myself, "If that's gay, then I'm joining that club."

Round Seven

Lewis kept on pouring punches down on Tyson, but the challenger was like a tank, seemingly impregnable. Lewis wanted to end it, he was trying to end it, but Tyson refused to submit. No man had ever absorbed so many of Lewis' blows. Tyson had never endured such a prolonged thrashing. It was another dominating round for Lewis.

As they pressed down on his facial injuries, Tyson winced and made a sound of pain. He looked like he was in agony. Tyson told Shields, with a hopeless resignation, "I can't get off."

Shields responded, "Let your hands go."

10-9, Lewis.

'If I start getting hurt and beat up, don't stop the fight. Let me get knocked out — like I knock them out. Don't stop it. Otherwise I'll knock you guys the fuck out." — Mike Tyson to his trainers in the gym before the Julius Francis fight (Source: Mario Costa)

Teddy Atlas:

I remember the first time Tyson came to the house. We'd seen him in the gym and already decided he'd come live with us after he got released on parole. He was spending his first weekend on good behavior, trying to impress everyone.

We were at this big oak table, full of food. The table was so heavy, it would take two people to move it. He was saying, Yessir, Nossir and all this crap. We knew it wasn't real.

He already showed he could punch like hell. That's all that mattered to Cus. Camille (Ewald) asked him to get a fork or spoon, which was behind him. He turned so quick—to show his obedience—his thigh was stuck on one of the divisions of the table. He picked up the whole thing. It was just funny to see everyone's reactions. Camille was going, Oh, my God!

Tyson was covering his face in shame, like he did something wrong. Cus was going, Look at that power! He don't know his own power! I'm watching all this like, look at these nuts.

∽ Round Eight ∾

Tyson shot out of his corner. He was making a final thrust. He threw a jab-right-left hook combo, but nothing scored. Lewis answered with a left hook-uppercut combo that buckled Tyson's knees badly. He froze again, just for an instant. Cotton separated the fighters, calling it a knockdown.

Tyson wobbled around, head down, right eye almost closed. The end was near now. Lewis resumed his attack. He was really unloading with full force.

"I was surprised and shocked at some of the punches he took," Lewis said later.

A final, perfect right hand was the deathblow. Tyson fell down on to his back, almost gracefully. He lay there, blood dripping from three different wounds—both eyes and his nose. He was finally beaten. It took a tremendous amount of punishment to finally subdue this man's will.

At the count of seven, Iron Mike laid his head back flat. Just for a second, though. Then he tried to get up. At ten, he was on one knee and still wobbling as he held out his right hand to grab a rope for support. The end came at 2:25.

Lewis tapped his right glove on his chest. He raised his hands high. He had finally proven his global fistic superiority. He was the best. No one in the world could deny it now. A former heavyweight champ declared on the US pay-per-view telecast, "Lewis is with no doubt the best heavyweight of all time. What he has done clearly puts him on top of the heap. He can do everything."

His partner at ringside agreed.

"He fought a virtually perfect fight, George. We just saw a masterpiece of a boxer-puncher in Lennox Lewis tonight."

In Las Vegas, Neiman said Muhammad Ali "…had a matter-of-fact expression on his face. The same look he always had after he won his fights."

Cotton helped Tyson across the ring. He put his left arm over Tyson's shoulders. Tyson leaned into him. He needed support to get back to his stool.

Will (Boxing fan from Rhode Island):

I went to the Freitas-Raheem fight at Foxwoods. Knowing Lennox Lewis was going to be at ringside, I brought one of my old *Ring* magazines with him on the cover, with hopes of getting an autograph by him.

So, after the fight I went ringside, but a lot of other people had the same idea as me. And Lennox wasn't really signing any autographs. So then Lennox left ringside, and a mob of people followed him. Having been to many fights at Foxwoods, I knew where he was going, so I made a beeline out of the bingo hall, and I waited at the door I thought he'd be coming through. I was the only one there, so I knew I might get lucky.

Sure enough, the door opens and Lennox comes through with a mob of people behind him. I held up my magazine and said, Excuse me, Lennox, you think I can get an autograph?

He grabbed the magazine from me, looked at it and said, This is a nice magazine. I'm going to keep this. And kept right on walking. Not even thinking, I started chasing him. What the hell! That's my magazine! To which he replied, My picture is on the cover, so it's mine.

Now I'm thinking, Man, this guy is a real jerk. Then he asked me for a pen and autographed it, and we both had a good laugh. He's a class act, made my night and gave me a great story to tell."

Tyson eventually walked over to congratulate his conqueror. Lewis saw him coming and met him halfway. Tyson said something into his ear. Lewis patted Tyson on his right shoulder just before being announced as the victor by Michael Buffer.

"…and still the undisputed Heavyweight Champion of the World…the pride of Great Britain — *Lennox Lewis*!"

XI

The Aftermath

How often does it happen that the greatest of talents are shrouded in obscurity.

— Plautus

Mike Tyson managed to shock the world again when it was all over. Nobody could have imagined that he would show sportsmanship and humility after being so decisively conquered. But Tyson was as gracious in losing as any great champion ever was. He may have won as much admiration in defeat as he ever had in victory.

Tyson stayed in the ring to do an interview, as Lewis stood nearby.

"Believe it or not, I know Lennox for, like, fifteen-sixteen years," Tyson said, looking at the champion. "We've always been friends. In competition, the best man has to win. We have to do everything we can. I'm happy for him to give me a fight. The payday was wonderful. I really appreciate it. And if you would be kind enough, I'd love to do it again. I think I could beat you if we do it one more time."

Tyson was asked why he thought he could defeat Lewis in a rematch.

"I explained before I need two or three more fights to get ready. He was just splendid. A masterful boxer, and I take my hat off to him. And if you give me one more chance, I'd be greatly appreciative."

Lewis, however, was not interested in an encore thrashing of the fallen legend.

"I just wanted to complete my legacy. Everybody said this fight is gonna count on my legacy. So I just wanted to prove to the people who is the best fighter in the world, on the planet. No guy tests this man.

"I showed boxing who is the best in the world. I showed that I'm a pugilist specialist. People thought I wasn't going to be able to deal with his style. But I was able to deal with it. I can adapt to any style. A lot of people thought he was going to be able to get away from my jab. But nobody gets away from my jab.

"I was really relaxed for this fight. I was so relaxed. I even started to worry myself...Am I too relaxed? But I was still cool. I felt really relaxed and positive."

Lewis was asked who would have won had the two fought a decade earlier. As Lewis began to answer, Tyson spotted some of his own blood on Lewis's left cheek. Iron Mike reached out and tenderly wiped it away.

Lewis did not acknowledge Tyson's surprisingly kind gesture as he answered, "Well, the funny thing about that is, heavyweights mature at different times. I would say when Mike Tyson was at nineteen, nothing would step in his way at that time. He ruled the planet at that time. But I'm like fine wine. I come along later on, and I learned my art and went along and I'm ruling now."

But a few weeks later Lewis would make a confession about having to fight the prime, vicious Mike Tyson of 1988.

"I hoped at the time I'd never have to fight Tyson, because he was an animal."

Mike was pressed again with the same question—Who would have won had they fought ten years ago?

"It wasn't meant to be. I've known Lennox since he was sixteen. I have mad respect for him. Everything I said was in proposition for promoting the fight. He knows I love him and his mother. And if he thinks I don't have respect and don't love him, he's crazy."

"He knows who I am. He knows I'm not disrespectful. I respect this man as a brother. He knows me ever since his [first trainer] Arnie brought us to Cus's together. And he knows I have much respect for him. Like I said before, he's a magnificent, a prolific fighter. And he should continue fighting."

About twenty minutes later, Tyson was in his dressing room holding his newborn son Miguel. He agreed to talk with HBO's Jim Lampley on camera. Tyson still seemed in a good mood, as if losing to Lewis was one of the best things that ever happened in his career. A blessing in disguise. Like he was somehow touched and then altered by Lewis' greatness.

It seemed as though an enormous pressure had finally been relieved. Maybe he had faced the realization and accepted that it was finally all over. Iron Mike Tyson could now just be Mike; he didn't have to live up to the image as the baddest man on the planet any longer. He even seemed to apologize for his misdeeds over the years.

"Lennox is a gentleman. I knew going into this fight I wasn't fighting a dirty fighter. And the reason I conducted myself like that [in the past]…I believe the fighters I fought—Botha, Norris, Holyfield—I believe they fought me a little dirty. And I guess I overdid some things and made it seem overt, that I have the reputation of a dirty fighter and it's okay. I've been through a lot, with Don King and these guys. And it just really transformed my behavior and my conduct. But things are going well now.

"But he just fought a wonderful fight. This guy… there's no way I could ever beat him. He's just too big and too strong. He's just a consummate fighter. And I just appreciate him giving me a shot fighting for the title. He fought great and basically wore me down. I could take a great shot. I just didn't see his punches.

"I've been friends with him for fifteen years. We're just like…I fly pigeons, right? This is a good equation. These pigeons live with each other for like ten, fifteen years. But when I throw feed down, they kill each other to get it. And it's the same thing with fighters. We love and respect each other. But we're like mercenaries, we need that money. We need to be the best. Money means nothing sometimes. But sometimes greatness is even more important than money."

Lampley asked Tyson again about a rematch.

"I don't know if I could beat him if he fights like that. But like I said, I'd fight him again. And I'll fight him with all the great aptitude to win. I will never quit. But I will fight to beat him."

Tyson talked about the possibility of retirement.

"Retire? It's up to the fighter. If he feels like he wants to retire, he should retire. But real fighters never really retire. We hang on to the last moment. We fight to eat as much as we can. You get your body beat as little as possible. You try to get as much as you can from your body."

Emanuel Steward agreed with Tyson's assessment that Lennox boxed a brilliant, near-perfect fight. He said, "The plan was exactly what Lennox did. He went out in the first round and established that he was not afraid of Mike. He stood toe-to-toe in kind of an alley fight situation for about a minute. Then, after that, he let Mike fight himself. And Lennox just grabbed him, tied him up. And at the end of the first round, Mike was a little more fatigued and also he had a little more respect for Lennox's punching power.

"But then Lennox came out for the second round and went into his battle plan, which was [to] make Mike fight at a distance. Where Mike couldn't fight. And once Mike got inside of that distance, Lennox shut him down and pushed him right back out there again. And kept working with his jab. Until he systematically destroyed him.

"Like, we watched Douglas-Tyson just prior to going to the arena. The thing that was interesting was that Buster carried the fight to Mike. The hammer jabs, not just alley fighting. Lennox did it. But I reminded Lennox of the fact that he punches a lot harder than Buster Douglas. And physically he's a much stronger man."

Lewis was asked about the controversial refereeing of Eddie Cotton.

"I definitely had another person against me. I was shocked that he was actually saying I was holding him. But I was just making sure he wasn't able to use his left arm, 'cause I noticed in previous fights, he usually comes up with an elbow or something. So I didn't want to fall prey to any of those kind of shots. So I kind of held his hand there, and that's the only thing I did. He was holding my left arm. Then the referee came in and warned me. I was really surprised.

"But it wasn't distracting for me. For a lot of good fighters, that can interrupt your focus. But for me, I was very focused on Mike. I didn't even let the ref bother me. I wasn't even looking at him. At one point in the fight he said, 'Look at me! Look at me!' And I still didn't look at him. I was really focused on Mike."

Steward was troubled by Cotton's suspicious officiating.

"He administered a standing-eight count [for the fourth-round knockdown]. Which we clearly made clear in the rules that there is no standing-eight counts. If you interfere, the fight is over with. You even noticed the demeanor of [Cotton]. It was really personal against Lennox. Never did he warn Mike. And the first warning [in the second round], you could see Mike in the clinch just telling him, He's holding me. The referee pushes Lennox out and then you see him offering Mike help.

"I was concerned about the referee. I never wanted to let Lennox know that because it would get him more agitated. I could see the referee was leaning towards Mike, towards trying to find any excuse to disqualify Lennox. And the longer the fight went on, I think the more the opportunities. I wanted Lennox to try and end it as much as possible."

HBO's Larry Merchant commented on the issue of Eddie Cotton: "There were conspiracy theories in midweek before the fight…that just such a scenario could unfold for various political reasons. And to see it as brazen as we saw it was quite remarkable."

Cotton wasn't the only unforeseen obstruction that Team Lewis had to overcome. The arrival of Panama Lewis to Memphis the week of the fight was ominous and unsettling. Though it didn't become known until after the fight just how chaotic Panama's influence nearly was.

"Panama Lewis is primarily known in boxing as a guy who does a lot of illegal things in boxing," Steward said. "He brings a lot of illegal substances, so to say. So, as a result, I only interpreted that he was brought in only to possibly do something illegal.

"And so as a result of that, I led the commission and everyone to believe that I would accept a urinalysis [drug test] from Tyson...before the fight. Which meant they could do that and take the illegal drugs and Mike would be fighting with that possibly. So to prevent that from possibly happening, at the very last minute, I told the commission I would not accept that and changed my mind. And that I insisted the drug test take place *after* the fight. So that way, whatever was in Mike Tyson's system would have to show up. And they were confused, there was a big, big argument over that. And finally we won. And that neutralized anything Panama Lewis could have done."

Tyson's camp offered no excuses for the performance of their man. Crocodile was in Hawaii with Tyson but was sent home for six weeks. He arrived in Memphis the week of the fight.

"I could tell when I got there, shit wasn't right. Like it should have been. Not taking anything away from Ronnie Shields or nobody, just wasn't our night. Mike wasn't himself that night. He wasn't there. After the first round, Mike told me he could never get his act together. He got hit in the first round — when he got hit by the first, clean right hand by Lewis. He never could recover after that, after the first round."

On the day of the fight, Crocodile said about Mike: "Mike was amped up and ready to go. It was subtle-like. It was a little heat but it wasn't a real, real lot of fire. But you could tell it was something he was gonna have to deal with. You could tell something wasn't right. Something wasn't right, you know what I mean? But it's just how the fight game goes, baby."

Trainer Ronnie Shields felt Mike was ready for Lewis. "We took all of Friday off. He was ready. He boxed a lot in the gym. He was in great shape. He was confident. I remember he told me, 'I really feel good. I'm ready to do this.' The day before the fight I told him to just relax and go over the gameplan, which was to stay close with Lennox, try and make him fight. Get inside, get inside Lennox Lewis's jab.

"The first round was good. But Mike got hurt in the second round real bad. Uppercut — it hurt him real bad. I don't think he ever recovered from that punch. Basically, things went down from there. He came back to the corner and said, 'I'm hurt. I want you to know I got hurt.' I said, Make sure you step around and step aside and attack behind your jab. Use your jab, good head movement and get inside.

"He tried his best. The type of warrior he is, he kept fighting. I think Mike did a great job. He did the best he could do. People got their money's worth.

"I was gonna stop it in the fifth, but I let those guys stop me. He was cut over both eyes. I take full responsibility, I should have stopped that fight. But I let them pressure me. We got caught up — [thinking] it's the old

Mike Tyson. He had a decent seventh round but in the eighth he got caught early, with a right uppercut. Before he got caught, me and Shelly were on the apron, trying to get the referee's attention. Right after that he got dropped."

Shields said he did not see Mike the day of the fight until early that evening.

"Mike stayed in the house with his bodyguards, manager, a lot of people, and I was at the hotel. Mike didn't want to stay at the hotel, he wanted a house. So they got a house for him. I was with him the day of...actually, I met him at the arena, about seven o'clock. At seven, he came to the arena with his sister and another girl — he had too many people around him, for me. Me, McKinley and Mike McCallum, we got there way early. We wanted to make sure the dressing room was exactly the way we wanted it to be. They had it perfect."

For slaying the dragon of Tyson, universal respect and recognition were now overflowing to Lewis. It would be a drastic reversal to the early days, when he received scant respect as the heavyweight division's seemingly unwanted stepchild.

I can recall two amusing examples that illustrate Lewis's misunderstood status of the early nineties. In 1994, I was present at the press conference at the Tavern on the Green in New York City's Central Park to announce Lennox's third title defense against Phil Jackson. After it was all over, I remember witnessing living legend boxing historian Bert Sugar conversing with Lewis right in the middle of the room, counseling him about how he should keep his fists up higher, even demonstrating several defensive poses.

Lewis, the good sport, politely acknowledged and played along with Sugar, who was once an amateur boxer and even sparred with Ali at Deer Lake in the seventies. It was a comical scene—here was the WBC Heavyweight Champion of the World taking fighting pointers from a boxing historian. Imagine Frank Sinatra accepting singing advice from a music critic.

But it portrays how under-appreciated and under-respected Lewis was at the time, and for so long after that.

Also, back in May of 1992, Lennox Lewis appeared as a guest on a British television show. He was seated next to WBC Featherweight Champion Paul Hodkinson, who had just defeated Steve Cruz by third-round TKO. At one point during the show, which was taped before a live studio audience, the host asked Lewis, "So, Lennox, who would you like to fight next?"

Lennox, who was 20-0 with 18 KO's at the time and fresh off a KO win over Derek Williams, answered, "It would be nice to fight Tyson next, but—"

Before he could finish his sentence, the studio audience erupted in spontaneous laughter. The host and Hodkinson had big grins on their faces and looked at Lewis like he was some kind of crazy fool. Like he had no chance whatsoever against Mike Tyson.

Now, ten years later, there was no one who could chuckle at or dispute Lewis's status as not only the greatest heavyweight of his era, but one of the finest of all time.

The world's newspaper headlines were finally saluting Lewis and his achievements:

LEWIS SHOWS TYSON, WORLD WHO'S CHAMP

—*The Boston Herald*

DOWN GOES TYSON

— Washington Times

LEWIS JUST TOO GOOD
FOR TYSON

— The Boston Globe

LEWIS HAS NOTHING
LEFT TO PROVE

— The New York Post

LEWIS LEAVES NO
DOUBTS

— The Arizona Republic

LEWIS BADDEST BULLY
ON THE PLANET

— The New York Post

LEWIS TAKES A BITE OUT
OF THE TYSON MYTH

— The Los Angeles Times

TYSON BATTERED,
BLOODIED, BEATEN

— The New York Daily News

LEWIS CONFIRMS HIS
LEGACY

— The London Times

TYSON SENT TUMBLING

— The New York Times

LEWIS DOMINATES
TYSON

— USA Today

LEWIS GETS REVENGE
AFTER GETTING BITTEN

— *Las Vegas Review-Journal*

David Williams of the Memphis *Commercial-Appeal*, captured the essence of the champion.

"We were told in the weeks leading up to June eighth, Lennox Lewis was a dull boxer and altogether a champion unworthy of clamor. We know him now, though, as a fighter with power, style, class…a pugilist specialist, as he told us."

None other than George Foreman hailed Lennox as the greatest ever.

"Lennox is beyond doubt the greatest heavyweight of all time. He is not second anymore. He is there at the top of the tree. He reminded me of a young George Foreman and an elusive Muhammad Ali. He has everything you want in a fighter."

XII

The Future

Be orderly and regular in your life so
that you may be violent and original
in your work.

— Flaubert

Lucia Rijker, the great female boxing champion who
would later have a prominent role in the Academy
Award-winning Best Picture for 2004, *Million Dollar
Baby*, articulated the enormous sociological and histori-
cal significance of Lewis vs. Tyson, perhaps better than
anyone.

"The other great fight in history — Louis-
Schmeling — was political. The fight of Lewis and Mike
was almost light against darkness. Good against evil.
And, to me, Mike needed the lesson to be humbled, he
needed the lesson to realize his causes and how he lived
his life were wrong. And Lennox was the one to show
him. And, to me, the fight represented that good wins
always over evil, eventually. Light wins over darkness.
That gave me hope...that there is justice in life.

"Because I thought fifty million dollars in the hands of a man that doesn't show responsible causes, would be dangerous. If Mike Tyson would have won against Lennox, he could have been a very dangerous influence. And if the world is like that, like Mike Tyson, where would the world go? It would be the world's destruction."

The fight was a bonanza for the city of Memphis. Lewis vs. Tyson was an all-around logistical and economic success. Mayor Herenton estimated it brought in upwards of $50,000,000 in revenues to Memphis. The announced attendance of 15,327 didn't quite fill up the 19,000-seat capacity of the Pyramid, even though ticket prices — which ranged from $2,400 to $250 — could be purchased at half of face value the day of the fight. But the pay-per-view figures were spectacular.

- Lewis-Tyson set records for highest grossing event in PPV history with an estimated $110 million in revenues from 2 million buys, which was not surpassed until 2007 by the Oscar De La Hoya-Floyd Mayweather event that sold a total of 2.4 million PPV buys at $54.95 and generated revenue of $134 million in the US.

- Lewis-Tyson also sold 760,000 pay-per-views in the UK. (De La Hoya-Mayweather sold 850,000 in the UK.)

- Lewis-Tyson set the record for highest gross gate revenues at $17.5 million, surpassing 1999's Lewis-Holyfield II's $16,860,300 at the Thomas and Mack Center in Las Vegas.

- HBO's rebroadcast of the fight a week later attracted a rating of 11, which according to TV experts was "incredibly high for a repeat showing."

- Tyson earned approximately $30 million in total after the PPV revenues were split.

- Lewis earned approximately $35 million (according to the Las Vegas *Review-Journal*), which was the largest purse in boxing history until De La Hoya earned about $45 million for losing a decision to Mayweather. (Some sources also estimate Tyson and Holyfield earned around $35 million each for "The Bite Fight.")

- The Lewis-Tyson 2 million PPV buyers' total revenue of $110 million dwarfed the record for a motion picture. It more than doubled the film record of $43.6 million grossed by the film *Spiderman* on its opening day in 2002.

More than 500 million fans from 130 countries — from Angola to Zimbabwe — had the option of watching Lewis-Tyson on pay-per-view or closed-circuit television, primarily in sports bars, theaters and restaurants. Memphis, the birthplace of FedEx, Holiday Inn and the home of Graceland, the city that launched B.B. King, Jerry Lee Lewis, Carl Perkins, Rufus Thomas, Otis Redding, Johnny Cash, Al Green, Booker T & the MG's and Elvis, the city where Dr. Martin Luther King was assassinated on April 4, 1968, now had a brand new distinction. Memphis was the home of one of the the biggest money fights in prizefight history. Memphis would forever be linked with Kinshasa, Zaire (Ali-Foreman), Manila (Ali-Frazier III), Yankee Stadium in the Bronx (Louis-Schmeling) and Madison Square Garden in New York (Frazier-Ali I), Jersey City NJ (Dempsey-Carpentier), Reno NV (Johnson-Jeffries) and New Orleans (Corbett-Sullivan) as one of the all-time most historically significant heavyweight title fight locations.

One of the last things Mike Tyson said before leaving Memphis was, "I'm just fortunate he didn't kill me in there. I don't have anywhere to go, nothing to do. I may just go to New York and feed my pigeons on the roof." But then later, he also quipped, "I just may go fade off into Bolivian."

Tyson always seems to be a contradiction—so strong and powerful yet so vulnerable at the same time. He could be so nasty the one day, yet so kind and gentle the next. He threatens to do all the wrong things but then ends up doing the right thing.

Maybe Mike Tyson can best be described by what his friends say about him—and not by what he did in the ring or what we saw, read and heard about his worst moments of behavior. Like Norman Mailer describes in *The Bullfighter*, "…a man cannot be judged by what he is every day, but only in his greatest moment, for that is where he shows what he was intended to be."

✜ Eddie Mustafa Muhammad (former WBA Light Heavyweight Champion): "I remember Mike when he was eight-years-old. Little big kid. He was always big, strong, tried to intimidate you. (*Even back then?*) It was the environment where we came from, that's all. Mike's always had a good heart. Always did have a good heart. Lot of fun, good people. Good people. Just a guy that liked to have fun.

The kids growing up in Brooklyn—like everybody else at the time—if you get out of line, your mother'd kick your ass. So everybody was in line.

(*When did you first realize Mike was a good boxer?*) It happened when he went away to reform school. Then you started hearing about Mike. A gentleman by the name of Bobby Stewart was training him at the time. They kept ranting and raving about Mike. But we all knew in Brooklyn what type of fighter he was. A lot of quality athletes come out of, not just Brooklyn, in Brownsville, that area—myself, Willie Randolph, Sly Williams, World B. Free, Ron Hagler—he used to play for the Detroit Pistons. We all came up in the same radius of two blocks

...I boxed with Mike. Mike had to be about nineteen. And I was at the tail-end of my career. Boxed for three rounds. Just spent one day up there [Catskills] because I wasn't doing anything that day. So I drove up—I was living in Woodbridge, NJ. After the sparring session was all over, he asked me, How did I do that? I said, I'm not gonna tell you because I may have to box you again [laughter]. I boxed his ears off. I wasn't gonna let this man hit me. I was, like, 180 pounds. It was a big ring. And I knew how to use the ring. When he got close, I tied him up.

(*What about his power?*) It's funny you should ask—the sparring partner before me, Mike knocked him out. Crushed him with a right hand. He was already warm.

(*Still friends with Mike?*) Sure, no doubt... Mike is at peace with himself now. Mike is a good person. He's a good person."

✤ Bobby Joe Young (former junior welterweight title challenger and the only man to defeat Aaron Pryor): "I used to know him all the time when I was in Jersey City working at Ringside. And Mike was there all the time. And we would talk, have conversations.

The thing that really impressed me about Mike is he had a very good respect for other fighters, the way he reveres a man, give you your dues. The benevolence — it's just really great. (*He knew you?*) Yeah. The first time I met Mike was in 1988. The fight when he knocked out Michael Spinks. I met him at the Garden. And he flipped when he met me. He said, *Bobby Joe Young!* He got excited. I was so blown away by how much he showed respect for me. Because I'm, like, I'm thinking to myself, I'm nothing compared to what you're doing, man. The way he reveres my accomplishments — it was really just a great respect I have for him.

People don't realize Mike Tyson. You're looking to be around good, honest people. He's so used to being around shysters, he don't know what their motives are. I think in that perspective, it's altered the way people think that he is. He's a nice guy. He really is.

✥ LeRoy Neiman: I've never known anyone who ever talked with or knew Mike Tyson that didn't have good things to say about him. Add me to that discriminating list. There was only one Dempsey, one Muhammad Ali, one Joe Louis, each his own man…so, too, only one Mike Tyson.

✥ Roberto Duran (boxing legend and idol of Tyson): My first memory when I met Tyson was when I went to his dressing room and he got crazy with me and was very happy to meet me. And I also appreciate him also. (*What fight?*) Michael Spinks. That was a helluva fight.

Mike asked me, "What one would be the quickest

way to knock Spinks out?" I said, "Punch him to the body, hook to the body." At the end of the fight, nobody could come to his dressing room, and when he knew it was me, he tell them to let me go in. And he said, "You see? I followed the way you told me. I was punching him in the body."

And the first time I went to Indianapolis, when I went to see him when he was in jail. I know Tyson — we're not the closest of friends — but with me he's a very, very good individual. The locations that we meet, he's very good with me, very nice. I remember one time he told me a story. I had a fight with Davey Moore (June 16, 1983). Tyson told me he was there in the gallery. At the time, Tyson was just a kid (16), nobody. But he was a fanatic of me.

Tyson told me he was shadowboxing up there in the shadows, screaming, "*Duran! Duran! Duran!*" Tyson told me that experience.

I consider that Tyson was the greatest boxer in the heavyweight. Because he was KO-ing anybody. Like nobody in history do what Tyson did. But also I consider that's the more important. His private life belong to — we talk about sport here. Tyson is/was one of the greatest. And no doubt to it. What happened was, when he was coming down, like anybody else — if Tyson rid of all the problems that he has, he can be champion, anytime.

What happened was, he had a lot of people, they take advantage of him, and also there was a personal problem. He don't love himself enough. I consider if he was loved a little more, with more ego, he can fight much better. Yeah, he can go back anytime.

∞ ∞

The loss to Lewis was not the end of Tyson's boxing career. After Lewis, Iron Mike got a large African tribal tattoo etched onto the left side of his face and defeated Clifford Etienne by first-round knockout in February 2003 in Memphis. In August, he declared bankruptcy — apparently having blown all of the approximately $300 million earned from his golden years. He told the Mexican press earlier in the year that he was broke and only "has $5,000 to his name. It's true that I lost all my money and that I have financial problems right now. But I am more happy now that I'm broke."

In July of 2004, the man who once shelled out $188,000 for two pet Siberian tigers stepped into the ring again — and lost by KO to little-known Brit Danny Williams, wiping out a lucrative title fight with new WBC champion Vitali Klitschko.

Tyson tried again in June of 2005, this time losing to the hulking but very mediocre Kevin McBride in Washington DC. Everything was gone now at age thirty-nine — the speed, the head movement, the passion…the fire. That Tyson fire that once had been a raging inferno, reduced to a flickering candle in the Lewis fight, was now completely out.

In that career-turning defeat to Lewis, Tyson reminded us, in many ways, of his great idol, former Heavyweight Champ Jack Dempsey. Dempsey — called "The Man Eater," "Kid Blackie" and "The Manassa Mauler" — was popular and infamous for having evoked widely ambivalent feelings from the public. Only after failure, at the end of his career, did Jack finally become one of the most beloved idols in American sports history.

The Tyson-Dempsey parallels are uncanny. Both were born in poverty and went on to capture the most coveted prize in sport. Both did it in spectacular style — Tyson by stopping Trevor Berbick in the second round, flooring him three times with a single blow, and Dempsey in utterly destroying giant Jess Willard so savagely that Willard suffered a broken jaw in two places, two cracked ribs, five teeth knocked out, one eye swelled shut and the hearing in one ear permanently impaired — all this destruction in only three rounds of boxing.

Both Tyson and Dempsey had unusually high-pitched voices. They both achieved dynamic championship reigns that transcended their popularities far beyond boxing. Both had colorful personalities, and they each married, and inevitably divorced, Hollywood movie stars — Tyson with Robin Givens, Dempsey with Estelle Taylor. Both were adored, resented, accepted and hated at the pinnacle of their careers. And both had to endure embarrassing court trials — Tyson for rape and Dempsey accused of draft dodging in the famous "slacker" trial, in which the key witness was his ex-wife, who was a prostitute.

At the end of his career, Dempsey was not cheered, but actually hooted as he entered the ring for his final fight as champion against Gene Tunney in front of over 120,000 spectators in Philadelphia in 1927. Father Time caught up to him that evening as Jack lost a decision to Tunney.

But Dempsey accepted the defeat and the end of his glorious championship reign with remarkable grace and dignity. I share this anecdote excerpt from Roger Kahn's masterpiece *A Flame of Pure Fire: Jack Dempsey and The Roaring 20's.*

"...At the final bell, Dempsey fought back the pain and threw an arm around Gene Tunney. 'Great fight, Gene,' Dempsey said. 'You won.' He walked back to his corner. The judges gave Tunney all ten rounds. In the corner, Dempsey heard cheering. People stood in the downpour and called his name. At last, some people were beginning to realize what they'd had. 'You'll always be the champion,' a man shouted. 'You're our champion forever!" He had never heard words like that in the ring before. Rugged Jack Dempsey blinked away tears. 'I want you to get to the people,' he told me 45 years later, 'that losing was the making of me.'"

Mike Tyson had many, many bad moments. Everybody knows that. But what should not be overshadowed is what he accomplished before the age of twenty-five. Mike Tyson should be most remembered for his greatest moment.

༄ ༄

Lennox Lewis arrived at Heathrow Airport in London on June 13. He declared his "Mission complete…I'm trying to bask in my glory. Enjoy it for a minute. There was always something to prove. Now that you've proven everything, you can relax."

When asked about his future plans, the champion wasn't sure.

"I don't see anybody out there that can beat me. It's just the young guys out there right now. There's nobody out there that can really give me a challenge."

Lewis took a year off after Memphis and eventually had one more fight in June of 2003, a TKO win over Vitali Klitschko in Los Angeles. He announced his retirement on February 6, 2004, in London.

"It's a special day in my life," he told the world's media. "I'd like to announce that June twenty-first, two thousand-three was my last fight as a professional boxer. It has been a great honor to be the standard-bearer of boxing for the last decade. Let the next era begin.

"I've completed all my goals, and now it's time for me to say goodbye. I definitely wanted to say goodbye at the top, and now I am at the top. I definitely will be the third boxer to retire as heavyweight champion, I promise you that. Mike Tyson was my ultimate fight. That was the fight that kept me around for a long time. I didn't want to go out without facing him. I didn't want people to say that Mike Tyson was the best around."

British bookmaker William Hill offered 7-2 odds that Lewis would fight again within two years.

The week of Lewis's farewell, Steve Brunt of the *Toronto Globe & Mail*, wrote this fine column regarding Lewis' legacy:

> He is the dominant heavyweight of the moment, perhaps eventually to be recognized as the best of his generation, and yet the paying public—especially the American paying public—doesn't really give a hoot.
>
> There are a variety of reasons for Lewis's lack of star quality, but to understand it fully, you have to go all the way back to a series of fights, the Riddick Bowe-Evander Holyfield trilogy. Those bouts, two won by Bowe and one by Holyfield, were indeed memorable moments for the sport. They defined both champions and made their reputations.
>
> They also, inadvertently, had an effect on the guy left looking

on from the outside—Lewis, who won the World Boxing Council portion of the world title after Bowe had discarded that belt in a trash can.

The television people, who for all intents and purposes run boxing, weren't really interested in having the Canadian/English Lewis as part of the mix. They didn't push for what would have been his own career-defining fight against his old Olympic rival, Bowe, or against a Holyfield closer to his prime.

They accepted Lewis as their primary meal ticket only after Bowe was gone, only after Tyson had self-destructed and after Holyfield had begun to slide. And even then, they did so reluctantly: it has seemed often that the interest wasn't in building Lewis, but in finding the next box-office attraction, the guy to beat Lewis, whether that was going to be Michael Grant or Wladimir Klitschko, or even David Tua.

When you really look at it, Lewis's career was one of the most impressive in heavyweight history. He beat every man he ever faced. And he brought style, grace and class to a sport that was thought to be a haven for hooligans. Lewis was a master scientific boxer blessed with knockout power in both fists. He was so versatile and so effective that he never suffered a pro-longed beating like many other greats. He was just too good and too smart and too dominant to have to engage in fights like that.

When his powers began to diminish, he realized it and accepted the truth. Using up his last bit of greatness in that dramatic and controversial victory over Klitschko, Lennox knew it was time to go at age 38. He exited the sport as champion with his wealth and health intact. And in the end, the game didn't defeat Lewis, leaving him helpless on the canvas, beaten and bloodied, like so many of the other greats. No, the lasting image of Lennox Lewis is as a winner. At the conclusion, the game didn't beat Lennox. Lennox beat the game.

Also remarkable about Lewis is how he was always a class act, through all the injustices and 'politricks' he had to overcome in the earlier days of his career. For the boxer, often the most challenging aspects of the sport are not always the battles con-fined to the ring. You have to swim with the sharks and constantly beware that you don't get eaten alive. Lewis survived so many obstacles and threats over 16 years, it's almost a miracle what the end result came to be.

Through it all, Lewis has never been arrested. Never been charged with any criminal con-duct. He never low-ered himself to calling an opponent an unprintable slur. Lewis brought a dignified respect to the noble art and sweet science. In many ways, he's been the personifica-tion of the quintessential boxing champion.

During his reign as champion, Lewis preferred to keep a low profile and kept much of his life private. As a result, he was generally considered unexciting, even dull by some. But in a modern world filled with so much violence and immorality, wasn't Lewis an outstanding role model for people to take inspiration from? He'll probably be respected in the future years much more than he was as the reigning champion.

I did this interview with Emanuel Steward in early 2006:

When was Lennox Lewis at his very best?

Emanuel Steward: "Oh, Lennox could be so unpredictable. I would say Botha, that was one of his greatest fights. Right about the time he fought Botha. He was sharp, precision. I mean, Lennox Lewis was a very good heavyweight.

But one of the things that I think a lot of people didn't realize about Lennox — Lennox physically was extremely, extremely strong. And guys who would fight him, and I would see them after, the first thing they would say is they were amazed at how physically strong he was.

And he blocked punches — it was just like hitting a big tree trunk or something, he would just push you off. Lennox was very physically strong.

And very unpredictable, even with us in the camp. We didn't know when Lennox would come out and just explode soon as the bell would ring. Or he would come out and be cautious. You never could tell about him. He's very unpredictable and explosive.

He was the best heavyweight I ever worked with.

When he was at his best, do you think there was any heavyweight in history who could beat him?

Steward: "When Lennox was at his very best he'd have been very difficult for anyone to beat. And I've said this a lot. The greatest heavyweight of all time was Muhammad Ali. And I will say Ali would have had problems with Lennox. Lennox was still taller than Ali. And Lennox had a very good left jab himself. But that's the closest anybody — not that he might have beaten Ali — but I think Ali would have beaten all the heavyweights in history, that I saw, still. But I think the ones he would have had the most trouble with were Lennox and Larry Holmes. Ali would have problems with Larry Holmes — in his prime. All of them in their prime. And he would have problems with Lennox Lewis.

What would your strategy have been for Lennox to execute against Ali at his best, you know, in the 1960s?

Steward: "Oh, talkin' about going against one of my favorites [smiles]. I would have Lennox to just pressure Ali and every time Ali jabbed, to pick the jab off and counter with a fast jab of his own. Being that Lennox was much taller, still taller than Ali. And physically strong. But make Ali throw a flickering jab and then block it real quick, then step back with a return jab.

Because Ali would oftentimes be off-balance up on his left leg when he would be jabbing, flicking. And nobody ever jabbed back to him much. But Lennox — being that he was taller than Ali — he'd have been over the top of Ali. Ali would have been trying to just pick and return real quick. And that would have kept Ali's timing and balance off. But the focus would have been on a jab contest. Outjabbing Ali, believe it or not.

But Ali was very…the one thing that was great about Ali… that I always said…all fighters that I've known in history pretty much…they had certain guys that they would fight certain styles, and they would always maneuver away from certain guys. Even Ray Robinson — I talked with George Gainford — he said we always had to keep Ray with guys about five-eight, and we never let him box too much with taller fighters. So the guy, even at his past best or whatever, he still had problems with Pender and Joey Archer even though he was older, but still, tall fighters bothered him.

But guys with jabs—he said maybe it was so much that Robinson could not handle jabs. [I said] "*Are you kidding?*" He said, "Nope." He said, "You look at the fights, even with Lamotta. Lamotta, literally—once in a while he'd come up with a little pick-pick jab, and Ray would get all unorganized.

He said Robinson had problems, just got disorientated with jabs. Even though he was always used to being the taller guy. So, if someone jabbed back, he got all unorganized.

And so we had Joe Louis. Joe, even in his prime, can't fight anyone that had movement, any trickiness, because Joe couldn't think if you started moving and tricking him. So, the Billy Conns and Walcotts and those guys, they were problems.

Ali fought everybody, I mean, just fought everybody. And the fights where his boxing style could not get him over the hump, he actually did say "I'll win this fight by just getting hit and landing three punches to every one." Kenny Norton and Joe Frazier and the guys he did have problems with their styles, Ali would just find a way to win. Even if it's "I gotta sit down and get hit and out-slug a guy and do this." That's why I always thought, in addition to his boxing skills, he was the greatest heavyweight.

But he would have had problems with Holmes and Lennox. Because a lot of the great boxers had problems with other guys who had jabs. So, that was the one punch that nobody threw at them much. So they had problems.

Which Lennox fight were you most concerned beforehand?

Steward: The least concerned fight was Mike Tyson. I never was concerned. Easy, easy, easy fight. And I even felt bad before that because Mike is one of my favorite fighters—and people, believe it or not.

Mike always had problems with big guys. And Lennox was trained to fight *as* a big guy, too. Not just to be bending down. And Lennox was not afraid of Mike.

So, based on all that, I knew that it was going to be an easy fight.

I would say the rematch fight with Rahman, because that's the guy that knocked out Lennox, and you never know what's gonna be on their mind. And I remember the rematch with Oliver McCall—I know he was still very tentative. I mean, very tentative. Even a few times when he could have knocked Oliver McCall out, Lennox was still tentative, would not take any chances. Would not become aggressive because maybe, you know, he would walk in [to something].

And going in there after he was knocked out by Rahman, he could have maybe had that same attitude. I guess the first time we went into that training camp after the Rahman fight, I remember the tension I could feel, and I'm in the ring with him, the whole camp was, like...everybody was, like, petrified—everybody, the trainers, his mom. And I remember the first time the guy threw a right hand and it missed him, I could hear everybody, like, was almost, like...I said, Whoooa.

And I didn't know how that was going to carry over to him too—when they were talkin' to him afterwards. But Lennox came through with a cocky, arrogant attitude, and he put on one of my records—"The Big Payback"—when he came in the ring. And he came in real, real arrogant and came through.

But that was the one I worried about. Because you don't know, whatever a guy may say or does in training camp before the fight; but until the moment of truth comes and the bell rings and he's facing the guy who knocked him out like that. You'll never, never know.

And it wasn't like Oliver McCall, when he got up right away at the count of three, and the referee stopped it kind of quick. With Rahman, he got crashed to the floor with a big powerful punch. So, that was the one I was worried about the most.

Boxing writer and New York-based lawyer Josh Dubin shared two anecdotes about Lewis, published in a *Boxing Digest* article in April 2004, that reveal the type of person he is, one whom most of the public never really got to know or embrace.

"...A few years ago, we had just arrived at the airport in New York," Courtney Shand (Lewis's fitness guru) told Dubin. "And we're standing outside, and some woman says to Lennox, "Just grab these bags and follow me to my car." She thought he worked as a luggage carrier, and..."

Shand cracks up laughing as the old memory comes back.

"Man, it was so funny. Lennox says to her, 'Absolutely,' and he grabs her bags and puts them on a cart and begins to roll it to her car. When he got to the car, he said to her, 'Sorry, I can't put your bags in the car because my ride is here.' And at that instant, I think it was the limo driver, but anyway, someone said, 'Mr. Lewis, your limo is here.'

"And you should have seen the look on the woman's face. You could tell that she recognized him, or at least knew that he was someone famous. He smiled at her and said, 'Have a lovely day.'

I remember the look on her face. She stood there very still as we got in the limo. When we drove away, she was still standing there with her jaw dropped open.

I don't know for sure, but I'd like to think that she changed her ways from that point forward. I know he definitely gave her something to think about."

Dubin had another story of Lennox at a lunch in Chinatown with lawyer Judd Burstein and manager Adrian Ogun.

"We're slurping won-ton soup and dipping egg rolls into duck sauce, talking about the differences between American and British fare," wrote Dubin. "Lennox is mid-sentence, mid-dunk, telling us his favorite foods, when a woman walks up to the table and infiltrates our conversation. She bypasses the conventional "excuse me," opting for the more subtle introduction of thrusting pen and torn piece of paper into his face.

"'Johnny. J-o-h-n-n-y—make it to Johnny,' she says, all snorty and nasally.

"I nearly choke on my food. Judd laughs aloud, and Adrian is stunned into silence. Lennox finishes chewing, and then says, 'I'm sorry ma'am. I usually don't turn people away, but…'

"'Come on, just sign it. It'll only take a second.'

"I look around for the cameras, because this has to be some sort of prank. One of those shows where they put a celebrity in a compromising situation to see how they'll react.

"'Excuse me,' he says, leaning toward her. 'Did you know that it's impolite to ask someone to sign an auto-graph while they're in the middle of a conversation, or the middle of a meal?'

'It'll only take a second.'

"I can see this is a lost cause. She hands him the pen, and he smiles. He signs his name—two swooshing Ls and a dot somewhere to the right of the second one. She snatches the piece of paper and rumbles back to her seat, mumbling 'thank you' with her back turned. A real piece of work, this lady.

"For the remainder of our meal, Lennox doesn't utter

a word. He pokes at his food a little and doesn't take another bite. He completely withdraws from the conversation. After fifteen minutes or so pass, I turn to him and ask if everything is all right?

"He says, 'Yes, everything is fine.' But he excuses himself from the table, walks across the restaurant and drags a chair from an empty table over to another table where a man and woman are eating lunch. I realize the woman he has joined is the one that had impolitely interrupted our meal just moments before. I turn my head and lean forward in a failed eavesdropping attempt.

"Before long, he has them both laughing — pounding the table and laughing. When he speaks, they beam like little children might in the presence of Santa Claus. He remains at the table for twenty minutes or so, and as he gets up to go, the woman rises and gives him a hug. I can read her lips when she says 'Thank you,' all drawn out and slow, her eyes sinking in appreciation.

"He tips his head to her, shakes the man's hand and struts back to our table.

"'What's for dessert?' he says as he sits down, and just like that he's back in the conversation, back to himself.

"I never asked him what he said to the woman, or what compelled him to go over and speak to her after she had been so unequivocally discourteous to him. It is almost as if there is something innate in this man, some divine force that won't allow him to be associated with a negative situation, no matter that it might be the ill-mannered behavior of others that give rise to it. In some ironic way, he sought to absolve the woman of her own actions by shining his light on her."

"That's Lennox, that's definitely Lennox," says

Courtney Shand. "That's just his attitude. He always knows how to turn a negative situation into a positive."

END

APPENDIX 1:
THE TALE OF THE TAPE

STATISTICS FOR LENNOX LEWIS AND MIKE TYSON AT THE TIME
OF THEIR CHAMPIONSHIP FIGHT

LENNOX LEWIS		MIKE TYSON
249.25	WEIGHT	234.5
6 ft. 5 in.	HEIGHT	5 ft. 11 ½ in.
84 in.	REACH	78 in.
44 in.	CHEST (NORMAL)	42 ½ in.
46 in.	CHEST (EXPANDED)	44 in.
17 in.	BICEPS	17 in.
15 in.	FOREARM	14 in.
34 in.	WAIST	34 in.
26 in.	THIGH	26 ½ in.
18 in.	CALF	17 in.
18 ½ in.	NECK	20 in
8 in.	WRIST	8 in.
12 in.	FIST	12 in.

LENNOX LEWIS		MIKE TYSON
36	AGE	35
Sep 2, 1965	BIRTH DATE	Jun 30, 1966
West Ham, Eng.	BIRTHPLACE	Brooklyn, NY
London, Eng.	HOMETOWN	Catskills, NY

APPENDIX 2:
COMPLETE LEWIS-TYSON
FIGHT CARD

TELEVISED

Lennox Lewis (39-2-1) vs. Mike Tyson (49-3), Heavyweight

Manny Pacquiao (33-2-1) vs. Jorge Eliecer Julio (44-3), Superbantam

Joel Casamayor (25-1) vs Juan Arias (33-2-1), Junior Lightweight

OTHER

David Starie (29-2) vs Ron Martinez (19-6-1, 15 KOs)
Super Middleweight

Malik Scott (10-0) vs Dan Ward (28-11-1)
Heavyweights

Jeff Lacy (9-0) vs Kevin Hall (18-5-1)
Super Middleweight

Nadel Hussein (24-1) vs Ronnie Longakit
Super Bantamweight

Cornelius Bundridge (11-0) vs Anthony Bowman (6-1-2)

Welterweights

George Klinesmith (11-5-1) vs Rico Hoye (7-0)
Light Heavyweight

Jo Ellen Wyman (8-4-1) vs Corrine Vanryck de Groot (9-0)

∽ ∾

APPENDIX 3:

The Record of Lennox Lewis

1989

6/27	Al Malcolm London, England KO-2 231
7/21	Bruce Johnson Atlantic City, NJ TKO-2 233
9/25	Andy Gerrard London, England TKO-4 235
10/10	Steve Garber Hull, England KO-1 232
11/5	Melvin Epps Kensington, England WDQ-2 230
12/18	Greg Gorrell Ontario, Canada TKO-5 226

1990

1/31	Noel Quarless London, England KO-2 225
3/22	Calvin Jones Gateshead, England KO-1 233
4/14	Mike Simuwelu London, England KO-1 233
5/9	Jorge Dascola London, England KO-1 232
5/20	Dan Murphy Sheffield, England TKO-6 230
6/27	Ossie Ocasio Kensington, England W-8 224
7/11	Mike Acey Ontario, Canada TKO-2 228
10/31	Jean Chanet London, England TKO-6 224
	Won European Heavyweight Title

1991

3/6	Gary Mason London, England TKO-6 227;
	Retained European Heavyweight Title

7/12   Mike Weaver Stateline, NV KO-6 221
9/30   Glenn McCrory Kensington, England KO-2 231
11/23   Tyrell Biggs Atlanta, GA TKO-3 235

1992

2/1   Levi Billups Las Vegas, NV W-10 225
4/30   Derek Williams Kensington, England KO-3 230
         Won British/Commonwealth
         Heavyweight Title
8/11   Mike Dixon Atlantic City, NJ TKO-4 233
10/31   Donovan Ruddock London, England KO-2 227

1993

5/8   Tony Tucker Las Vegas, NV W-12 235
         Retained WBC Heavyweight Title
10/1   Frank Bruno Cardiff, Wales TKO-7 229
         Retained WBC Heavyweight Title

1994

5/6   Phil Jackson Atlantic City, NJ KO-8 235
         Retained WBC Heavyweight Title
9/24   Oliver McCall London, England L TKO- 2 238
         Lost WBC Heavyweight Title

1995

5/13   Lionel Butler Sacramento, CA KO-5 248
         Won WBC Heavyweight
         Elimination Bout
7/2   Justin Fortune Dublin, Ireland TKO-4 246
10/7   Tommy Morrison Atlantic City, NJ TKO-6 241

1996

5/10   Ray Mercer New York, NY W-10 247

2/7   Oliver McCall Las Vegas, NV TKO-5 251
        Won WBC Heavyweight Title
7/12   Henry Akinwande Lake Tahoe, NV WDQ-5 242
        Retained WBC Heavyweight Title
10/4   Andrew Golota Atlantic City, NJ TKO-1 244
        Retained WBC Heavyweight Title

1998

3/28   Shannon Briggs Atlantic City, NJ TKO-5 243
        Retained WBC Heavyweight Title
9/26   Zeljko Mavrovic Uncasville, CT W-12 243
        Retained WBC Heavyweight Title

1999

3/13   Evander Holyfield New York, NY Draw 12 246
        Retained WBC Heavyweight Title
11/20   Evander Holyfield Las Vegas, NV W-12 242
        Won Undisputed Heavyweight Title

2000

4/29   Michael Grant New York, NY KO 2 247
        **Retained undisputed world
        heavyweight title**
7/15   Frans Botha London, England TKO 2 250
        **Retained WBC-IBF
        heavyweight titles**
11/11   David Tua Las Vegas, NV W 12 249
        **Retained WBC-IBF
        heavyweight titles**

2001

4/22   Hasim Rahman South Africa, L KO5 253
Lost WBC-IBF
heavyweight titles
Nov. 17 Hasim Rahman Las Vegas, NV KO 4 246
Won WBC-IBF
heavyweight titles

2002

6/8   Mike Tyson Memphis, TN KO 8 249 1/4
Retained WBC-IBF
heavyweight titles

2003

6/21   Vitali Klitschko Los Angeles TKO 6 256 1/2
Retained WBC heavyweight title

Fights:	44
Wins:	41
Losses:	2
Draws:	1
KO's:	32

APPENDIX 4:

The Record of Iron Mike Tyson

1985

3/6	Hector Mercedes Albany, NY KO- 1 214
4/10	Trent Singleton Albany, NY KO- 1 214
5/23	Donald Halpern Albany, NY KO- 4 212
6/20	Rick Spain Atlantic City, NJ KO- 1 217
7/11	John Alderson Atlantic City, NJ KO- 1 215
7/19	Larry Sims Poughkeepsie, NY KO- 3 217
8/15	Lorenzo Canady Atlantic City, NJ KO- 1 214
9/5	Mike Johnson Atlantic City, NJ KO- 1 219
10/9	Donnie Long Atlantic City, NJ KO- 1 215
10/25	Robert Colay Atlantic City, NJ KO- 1 217
11/1	Sterling Benjamin Latham, NY KO- 1 221
11/13	Eddie Richardson Houston, TX KO- 1 219
11/22	Conroy Nelson Albany, NY KO- 2 221
12/6	Sammy Scaff New York, NY KO- 1 215
12/27	Mark Young Latham, NY KO- 1 216

1986

1/11	David Jaco Albany, NY KO- 1 217
1/24	Mike Jamison Atlantic City, NJ KO- 5 215
2/16	Jesse Ferguson Troy, NY KO- 6 217
3/10	Steve Zouski Uniondale, NY KO- 3 220

5/3	James Tillis Glen Falls, NY W- 10 215
5/20	Mitch Green New York, NY W- 10 215
6/13	Reggie Gross New York, NY TKO- 1 217
6/28	William Hosea Troy, NY KO- 1 217
7/11	Lorenzo Boyd Swan Lake, NY KO- 2 219
7/26	Marvis Frazier Glen Falls, NY KO- 1 217
8/17	Jose Ribalta Atlantic City, NJ KO- 10 213
9/6	Alfonso Ratliff Las Vegas, NV KO- 2 221
11/22	Trevor Berbick Las Vegas, NV KO- 2 221
	Won WBC Heavyweight Title

1987

3/3	Bonecrusher Smith Las Vegas, NV W- 12 219
	Won WBA Heavyweight Title
	Retained WBC Title
5/30	Pinklon Thomas Las Vegas, NV KO — 6 218
	Retained WBA-WBC
	Heavyweight Titles
8/1	Tony Tucker Las Vegas, NV W- 12 221
	Won IBF Heavyweight Title
	Retained WBA-WBC Titles
10/16	Tyrell Biggs Atlantic City, NJ KO- 7 216
	Retained WBA-WBC-IBF
	Heavyweight Titles

1988

1/22	Larry Holmes Atlantic City, NJ KO- 4 215
	Retained WBA-WBC-IBF
	Heavyweight Titles
3/21	Tony Tubbs Tokyo, Japan KO- 2 216
	Retained WBA-WBC-IBF
	Heavyweight Titles
6/27	Michael Spinks Atlantic City, NJ KO- 4 218
	Retained WBA-WBC-IBF

Heavyweight Titles

1989

2/25	Frank Bruno Las Vegas, NV KO- 5 218
	Retained WBA-WBC-IBF
	Heavyweight Titles
7/21	Carl Williams Atlantic City, NJ KO- 1 219
	Retained WBA-WBC-IBF
	Heavyweight Titles

1990

2/11	Buster Douglas Tokyo, Japan L KO- 10, 220
	Lost WBA-WBC-IBF
	Heavyweight Titles
6/16	Henry Tillman Las Vegas, NV KO- 1 217
12/8	Alex Stewart Atlantic City, NJ KO- 1 217

1991

3/18	Razor Ruddock Las Vegas, NV KO- 7 217
6/28	Razor Ruddock Las Vegas, NV W-12 216

1992-1994 Inactive

1995

8/19	Peter McNeeley Las Vegas, NV WDQ- 1 220
12/16	Buster Mathis Jr. Philadelphia, PA KO- 3 219

1996

3/16	Frank Bruno Las Vegas, NV TKO- 3 220
	Won WBC Heavyweight Title
9/7	Bruce Seldon Las Vegas, NV KO- 1 219
	Won WBA Heavyweight Title
9/24	Stripped of WBC Title for not fighting man-

datory challenger Lennox Lewis

11/9   Evander Holyfield Las Vegas, NV L KO- 11 222
       Lost WBA Heavyweight Title

1997

6/28   Evander Holyfield Las Vegas, NV LDQ- 3 218
       For WBA Heavyweight Title

1998 Inactive

1999

1/16   Francois Botha Las Vegas, NV KO- 5 223
10/23 Orlin Norris Las Vegas, NV NC- 1 223

2000

1/23   Julius Francis Manchester, England KO- 2 223
6/24   Lou Savarese Glasgow, Scotland KO- 1 222
10/20 Andrew Golota Detroit, Michigan TKO- 3 222

2001

10/13 Brian Nielsen Copenhagen, Denmark TKO- 7
       239

2002

6/8   Lennox Lewis Memphis, TN L KO- 6 234
       For WBC-IBF Heavyweight title

2003

2/22   Clifford Etienne Memphis, TN KO-1 225 3/4

2004

7/30   Danny Williams Louisville, KY L KO- 4 233

2005

6/11   Kevin McBride Washington, DC L TKO- 6 233

Fights:	58
Wins:	50
Losses:	6
No Contest:	2
Draws:	0
KOs:	44

Appendix 5:
Lennox Lewis Interview
May 2006

Scoop: Do you remember the next time you saw Mike Tyson after that sparring session in the Catskills?

Lennox Lewis: The next time I saw him was on TV, he was at the Olympics in 1984. He was at ringside watching fights. When I was fighting Tyrell Biggs, Tyson was telling me at ringside to hit him to the ribs. We always had a mutual respect for each other since we sparred those early times. We got that over with.

Scoop: Do you remember Tyson showed up at your public workout at Grand Central Station in New York City before the David Tua fight for, like, two minutes? Why do you think he did?

Lennox Lewis: You remember that one? That was weird. I don't know why he came. He was welcome to come watch. I was lookin' good in sparring that day [smiles]. I remember someone said, "There's Tyson." I looked over and couldn't see him. I just saw a crowd of people. I thought, What's he doing over there?

Scoop: Do you remember when you first got the idea in your head that you could actually become the world heavyweight champion?

Lennox Lewis: For me, it was a long journey. I realized it was going to be lots of curves and bumps and hills—I just wanted to make it to the top. In the amatuers, it was the Eastern Germans, Russians and Cubans. I had to try to find the way to beat each one. What's his weakness? Go to the body. Then I'd try that way to beat them. This guy can't take a right hand. Then I'd just train that way to beat him. My fear was losing. How do I win? How do I prepare to win? Then I would prepare in this manner.

Tyson didn't have an extensive [international] amateur career like I did. A lot of people don't realize how that helps you. I'll try to put it like this: after about twenty-five fights you don't always have to keep going to the bathroom before the fight. Then after you get over that, you still get the butterflies before the fight. Then you eventually get over that and the butterflies are gone. You no longer get nervous or scared before fights. Then you have enough experience where, before the fight, you can start to break down the fights—What do I need to do? How do I beat him?

Scoop: Who was the most talented boxer you faced?

Lennox Lewis: [Pause]…I don't know. It's funny. Razor Ruddock was real talented, when I first came on the scene. He had a great jab. He had an excellent jab. It was like a right hand. He actually was a converted southpaw. But then he started lifting weights and his style changed.

Scoop: How did the public's treatment of you change after the Tyson fight?

Lennox Lewis: The main thing about that—I was trying to retire a year before. But I couldn't because I never fought Tyson. For us to never have met, people would always say if I was like getting a haircut—Yo, you never fought Tyson. I was stuck on that image of Tyson. I had to fight him. In a sense, it's kind of weird. A lot of fans said I should give him another chance, they want to see it again. I'm like, They want to see that fight again?! They felt that Tyson wasn't right, if he trained longer he'd do better. The way I see it is, when I saw Tyson knocking everybody out on TV, I thought, He's goooood. But when I saw him in person, he didn't look as awesome. It's like in the amateurs. Fighters used to be afraid of the Russians, Cubans, but then I'd figure them out and figure out how to beat them. Tyson was the same way. As good as he was, he was always more one-dimensional. I was five-dimensional.

Scoop: An aspect of your fight with Tyson is that, in a sense, it really was a confrontation between good and evil. At the time, the way Tyson was behaving and living his life, he was almost a symbol of evil. And your reputation was always very good and positive. Did you feel that extra pressure to prevent evil from triumphing? And the influence it would have had on society to see a man like Tyson rewarded with around $100,000,000 if he beat you?

Lennox Lewis: There was a big thing like that. He helped with that. He just made me train harder. The Tyson fight was, like, the hardest I ever trained for a fight in my entire career. The press conference in New York, when he bit on my leg, I was mad. I came to promote the fight wearing a two thousand-dollar suit, and he bit me on the leg. And I couldn't say anything. Because if I said something, it would look like maybe I didn't want the fight. But then I realized he was just trying to take the sucker's way out. I'm not saying I know the person from the outside, that's how it looked to me. Then the guy surrounded himself with kind of illin' people—Who's that guy who did the dirty stuff? (Panama Lewis.) I thought, They can't come to the ring with him. These guys aren't going to fight for him. He mentally needs them to get him going. If he needs them, then he's at a weakpoint.

Scoop: When you and Tyson are in the ring, you two had a pretty long staredown. What did you see in his eyes?

Lennox Lewis: He had to come up to the human line to look at me. My body was hard, and I hit it, I was saying, like, Come and hit it. I was very confident. I just looked at the Buster Douglas fight. That's the only fight I need to see. He didn't become Superman after that fight. He only deteriorated.

Scoop: What was your last meal before the fight?

Lennox Lewis: Spaghetti [with red sauce].

Scoop: In the fight did Tyson do anything that you did not expect?

Lennox Lewis: I'm glad that he fought fair. Because I was definitely ready for anything. Even after [the fight], I had respect for him. I was hitting him with some shots. It was the first fight where my hands were a little sore. I said it was because of the size of that neck. He's like a shock absorber. He'd take it, shake it off and come back at you. Like that Rhino Man in *Spiderman* [cartoons].

Scoop: I remember at the Cory Spinks-Ricardo May-

orga fight in Atlantic City in December of 2003 you and Tyson were at ringside watching the fights in the same area, with him one seat in front of you. I was wondering if you both talked at all that night?

Lennox Lewis: Yeah. I don't know. For me, there's never any bad blood—unless you do something to me. When we sat there, everyone was tense, looking at us, everybody was tense like that. I could tell. I said, What's goin' on Mike? He looks back at me, [says in a highstrung voice], What's goin' on with *you*? And that was it [laughs]."

Scoop: In what fights were you at your very best? When did you feel the best in the ring, the sharpest?

Lennox Lewis: Definitely the Tyson fight. Rahman fight. Tucker. Holyfield [first]. I think the aftershock of the first fight affected the second fight. I thought, *I won, but now I have to win again?*

Scoop: When do you think Tyson was at his very best?

Lennox Lewis: I'd have to say even before I turned professional. He was like a whirlwind, knocking everyone out. At that point, he was at his best. I think the environment affected him. Coming from nothing to suddenly having millions, and having everybody adoring him…you know, I'm an analyst. I analyze everything. Even his relationship with Robin Givens helped me. She helped a lot of athletes. It showed there was those types of woman out there, watch out. Playin' the game, it's only one thing they want. That's all I want to say about that. But Emanuel Steward said Tyson was going to be my easiest fight. I was like, Really? I never let myself think that until after the fight.

Scoop: Who are some of your famous fans? Who have you met that admires you?

Lennox Lewis: It's like this: I was over at the Cannes Film Festival one year. We were walking in from the beach, on an elevator. Robert Goulet comes over. "Hey, Lennox Lewis, how you doing?" I'm, like, starstruck. I had just watched him in a movie the other day. Puff Daddy—I remember they asked him who he picked in the fight with Tyson. He says, "I'm going with Tyson because he's from New York." I say to myself, *That's why you're pickin' Tyson? Because he's from New York? Not on styles?* I saw him later. So, I asked him, "Who's gonna win?" He says, "Tyson's my man. I know you got better skills but Tyson's my man."

Another time I see Spike Lee. I'm thinking maybe we can get together, maybe he can put me in a movie of his. Then all of the sudden I see Spike Lee running through the crowd, like, jumping over tables—to get over to shake Mike Tyson's hand. I'm, like, There goes my part in the movie!

But I come across famous people all the time. It's the respect factor I appreciate. They respect me, they respect what I've achieved and the manner I've done it. It's street credibility. They know where I'm coming from, they know my reputation.

Appendix 6
The Biofile: Lennox Lewis
By Scoop Malinowski

Childhood Hero: Muhammad Ali.

Hobbies/Interests: Now, because I have the time, I look at myself as an entrepreneur, whether it's training, promoting or having my own store—it's endless what I can do. I play a lot of chess. I'm starting to play poker now, I like Texas hold 'em. I play tennis almost every day.

Nicknames: Lennie The Lion, Lennox "Lethal" Lewis, The Gentle Giant, Rough & Rugged, Cool & Deadly.

Favorite Movie: *Dune.*

Favorite TV Shows: Sci-Fi Channel.

Musical Tastes: Hardcore reggae—Capleton and Sizzler, Beanie Man.

Favorite Meal: Jerk chicken.

Favorite Ice Cream Flavor: Rum Raisin.

Childhood Dream: [To be a] Fireman.

Pre-Fight Feeling: Very focused. You mustn't let your mind wander on to anything else when you're boxing. If you're not concentrating one-hundred percent, you're courting disaster. There's a man across the ring trying to take the top of your head off. The only fear I have is the fear of losing. I don't feel fear or pain or fear of my opponent, because I have prepared myself to deal with anything that happens in a fight. Boxing is the life I've chosen and the risk I've decided to take. It's like when people climb Everest and then suddenly five of them fall off the mountain and die. And people are asking, Why, why? Well, just because—because we're human beings, and we test ourselves with challenges.

First Job: Shoveling snow in Kitchener, Ontario, Canada. I was an entrepreneur [smiles].

First Car: A big, old boat, I don't know what it was [smiles].

Early Boxing Memory: When I was a kid and I was running I would sometimes fantasize about boxing. But in an odd way, I was never Muhammad Ali. It was always me fighting his fights. On those runs, I must have knocked out George Foreman and Joe Frazier a hundred times in my imagination. But it was always me, doing it my way, never Ali doing it his.

Greatest Sports Moment: Olympics (1988 in Seoul, Korea). It was the heart of my amateur career and the start of my professional career. When I stepped in the ring for the first fight, people didn't know much about me. They thought I was a guy that might make it to the final. After the fight (vs. Bowe for the gold medal), they wanted to take my picture, were asking for autographs. I was at the top of the hill. Now there's another one ahead.

Most Painful Moment: I think when I hurt my thumb playing football [smiles]. I guess my first defeat. I never expected to get knocked down. I got knocked down and lost the fight. Hated that.

Worst Injury: Punching the body, catching his elbow. (Against who?) Some guy in sparring.

Embarrassing Boxing Memory: No.

Favorite Vacation Spot: Jamaica.

Favorite Boxers To Watch: I like Mayweather. Winky Wright. Jermain Taylor. I like all those guys—I like the talented boxers.

People Qualities Most Admired: Just being truthful. Honest. Helpful. I like characters.

Sources

"World Heavyweight Champion and Not Just of Boxing;" © Josh Dubin, *Boxing Digest*; April 2004. Used by permission

Bad Intentions: The Mike Tyson Story; Peter Heller; 978-0306806698; Da Capo Press, 1988; p 63, 66, 80. Used by permission.

Lennox Lewis Champion; Lennox Lewis with Ken Gorman. Faber and Faber Limited, 1993; p. 38, 39, 53, 54; © The Estate. Used by permission

Max Schmeling: An Autobiography; translated and edited By George Von Der Lippe; 978-1566251082; Bonus Books Inc., 1977; p 11. Used by permission

By George: The Autobiography of George Foreman; George Foreman and Joel Engel; 978-0679443940; Villard Books, 1995; p. 67. Used by permission

Chaos, Corruption, Courage and Glory; Thomas Hauser; Sports Media Publishing Inc.; 2005. © Thomas Hauser. Used by permission.

ABOUT THE AUTHOR

SCOOP MALINOWSKI, born in Philadelphia, has written about boxing for *The New York Post*, *The New York Daily News*, CBSsportline.com, *The Ring*, *Boxing Digest*, *World Boxing*, *Boxing Update* newsletter, *Boxing News* (U.K.) *World Boxing* (Japan), *The Fist* (Australia), *Boxing World* (South Africa), *Boxing Illustrated*, Don King Productions, and at Boxinginsider.com, Boxingtalk.com, Fightnews.com and Eastsideboxing.com.

ABOUT THE ARTIST

ANGELA WATERS: My eclectic tastes in music and books have converged with my fascination with technology. Sleepless nights are filled with listening to hardcore rockers and playing out the tunes in colors that describe my vision of an author's words. My muse is thrilled it finally has a place to cut loose.

Printed in the United States
126269LV00003BA/1/P